Rail Trails: South West

Rail Trails : South West

Essays in steam

A selection of the popular 'Rail Trail' articles from the
Torquay *Herald Express*

Peter W. Gray

Silver Link Publishing Ltd

These articles were first published in the regular Saturday feature 'Rail Trail' in the Torquay *Herald Express* between 1985 and 1991, and are reproduced by kind permission of the Editor.

First published in book form in October 1992
Reprinted February 1993
Paperback edition first published in June 1996

British Library Cataloguing in Publication Data

Gray, Peter W.
      Rail Trails: South West - Essays in Steam
      I. Title
      385.09423

ISBN 0 947971 94 7 (Hardback)
ISBN 1 85794 067 9 (Paperback)

Silver Link Publishing Ltd
Unit 5, Home Farm Close
Church Street
Wadenhoe
Peterborough PE8 5TE

Tel/fax 01832 720440

Printed and bound in Great Britain

Introduction

Many years ago I recall my father telling me about his younger days when he started work for the Great Western Railway at Paddington, and travelled up from Southall every day during the pre-1914 period. The railways were then at the height of their splendour and I envied him the sights he could describe, and wished at the time that I could have been born 30 years earlier.

With the passing of the years I now realise that I too was privileged to have been around and actively recording railway events here in the South West during the post-war years - a period now recalled with affection by many of those who were either not so fortunately placed, or who were too young to do anything about it. So when, in late 1984, with the 1985 celebrations of the GWR's 150th anniversary in mind, Jim Mitchell, the Editor of our local evening newspaper, the Torquay *Herald Express*, invited me to contribute a weekly captioned photograph for the Saturday feature page, I had no hesitation in accepting.

For me it was an opportunity to share with the general readership of the paper my interest in railways, and to explore week by week some of the events which I had recorded many years ago, sketching in the historical background, or explaining the operations taking place.

I have been encouraged by the interest shown, often by people with only a marginal interest in railways, though I have written with them in mind, rather than the dedicated railway enthusiast. Nevertheless, the articles seem also to appeal to enthusiasts, and are widely collected, cut out and passed from person to person, one copy even reaching New Zealand each week.

Working to a weekly deadline means that unless the original source material is readily to hand, I have to rely on already published material. I must, therefore, acknowledge here my deep debt of gratitude to all those authors of books about the West Country and its railways, from whose earlier researches I have culled the odd fact here and there - and most of whose books I have purchased.

With the exception of the pre-war views on the sea wall at Dawlish and Teignmouth, which are from my collection, all the photographs are my own. They were taken using, successively, three different cameras, all of the folding bellows type. Until early 1955 I had an early post-war French Kinax with a Berthiot lens and a primitive viewfinder, which only performed reasonably well under good conditions. In 1955 this was changed for a pre-war Super Ikonta with a Tessar lens, which gave an immediate boost to photo output, and in 1957 a final change was made to the Voightlander Bessa II with Heliar lens, on which most subsequent black and white exposures were made.

In the preparation of these articles, wherever possible facts have been carefully checked, and memory not relied upon to any extent, but if there are any errors I can only apologise.

The selection of the 92 pictures for this book, from the more than 350 which have already been published in the *Herald Express*, was a difficult task. Many that I would have liked to include have fallen by the wayside for various technical reasons, but could be included in a further volume, should one be demanded.

Lastly, a big 'thank you' to Jim Mitchell, Editor of the *Herald Express*, both for starting it all off and for giving me complete freedom as to which subject I tackle each week.

Peter W. Gray
Torquay

Rail Trails: South West

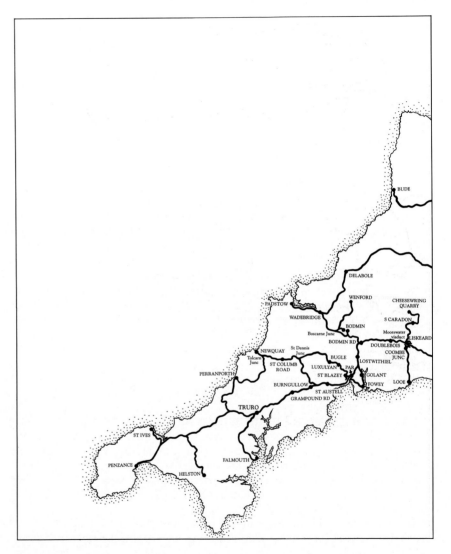

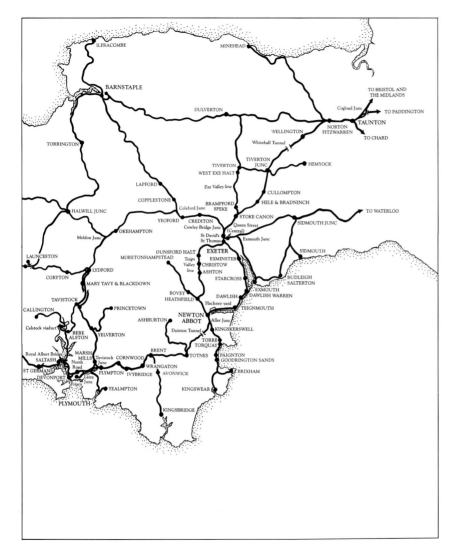

Map of the railways of Devon and Cornwall showing locations featured in the book or mentioned in the text. Christina Siviter

City of Truro

One of the most famous GWR locomotives ever to grace our metals, the 4-4-0 No 3440 *City of Truro*, is seen here shortly after her arrival back at Newton Abbot after hauling an eight-coach excursion train from Swindon to Kingswear on 19 May 1957; this was one of her first long journeys following restoration to running order at Swindon Works after 26 years in the original LNER railway museum at York. On the footplate is Divisional Locomotive Inspector Frank Weaver.

'Why is *City of Truro* so famous?' some may ask. Certainly not because of any startling new design features incorporated when she was built at Swindon in 1903. In fact she was something of a hybrid, with a new Churchward-designed taper boiler, with its high, cornered Belpaire firebox, mounted on a rather old-fashioned double frame chassis, which was a design considered obsolete even in 1903.

Her fame arose from a single journey on 9 May 1904 conveying mail from Plymouth to Bristol, including gold bullion payment for the Panama Canal, which had arrived at Plymouth that morning aboard the Norddeutscher Lloyd liner *Kronprinz Wilhelm*. From Bristol the mail train was taken over by Dean 'Single' No 3065 *Duke of Connaught* for the remainder of the journey to Paddington.

City of Truro's contribution was a very fast run over the tortuous South Devon banks, in a time which can barely be equalled by today's High Speed Trains, and an even more amazing descent of Wellington bank, where she became the first locomotive, and possibly the first vehicle in the world, to achieve the magic 100 miles per hour *and* be reliably timed while doing so.

One of the strangest features of this remarkable run was that although the GWR took full advantage of the publicity of this very fast run at the time, it was not until 1922, 18 years later, that they allowed the maximum speed to be published! Perhaps in 1904 the company's management were fearful that many of their regular travellers might share the then only recently deceased Queen Victoria's well-known distaste for high speed when travelling in the Royal Train.

In the background of this picture, Newton Abbot station, shed and the Locomotive Factory are virtually unchanged since Great Western days. The shed has recently acquired a new roof, but the other fruits of the 1955 Modernisation Programme have yet to appear.

The west end pilot engine, probably 0-6-0T No 9462, is about to remove some empty stock from platform No 6 and behind the coal stage, with its rarely used wartime extension, stands the Factory weather-vane, cut out in the shape of a broad gauge single-wheeler.

7 September 1985

No 100

The westerly breeze blows leaking steam across to the fireman's side of No 6008 *King James II* as the loco proudly makes the final assault on the last 100 yards of Dainton bank with train number 100, the 5.30 am from Paddington, on 29 October 1955.

The 5.30 am Paddington to Penzance was a GWR institution which almost certainly existed for as long a period of years as the company and, because it continued to run for another 20 years after the GWR ceased to exist at the end of 1947, may well have run for more years than the GWR lasted.

Known as 'The Parliamentary', it probably dated from the 'Cheap Trains Act' of 1844, which decreed that each railway company must run at least one passenger train each day conveying 3rd class passengers in covered vehicles. Prior to this Act, the GWR was not alone among railway companies in keeping its passenger trains for the gentry to travel in at 1st or 2nd class rates. Anyone rash enough to wish to travel 3rd class was conveyed in open wagons with bench seats, attached to goods trains. Mind you, we 3rd class passengers must have been a pretty rough lot in those days, in our smocks and clay pipes, or clogs and shawls, with a fair sprinkling of Irish navvies and their families roaming from contract to contract on the railways that their muscles had largely helped to build.

With such people in mind, the GWR may have considered itself justified in starting the train they were compelled to run for their 3rd class passengers at such an inconvenient hour as 5.30 am, as this would ensure they were well out of the way by the time any regular business people arrived.

Never a particularly fast train, in broad gauge days, before 1892, it arrived at Newton Abbot at 12.48 pm, and after reversing at Plymouth Millbay and stopping at all Cornish stations, it eventually staggered into Penzance at 6.25 pm. On the way, it stopped at Kingsbridge Road (later renamed Wrangaton) to connect with the horse-drawn coach to the South Hams.

The 5.30 am Paddington's finest hour came in 1902, when it was included in the general improvement of GWR schedules to such effect that a three-hour improvement in the arrival time at Penzance was achieved.

Thereafter, apart from a slowing down during the war, it continued to arrive at Newton Abbot around 11.30 am, and Penzance at 4.25 pm, until 1960. With the arrival of more powerful diesel locomotives to replace the steam engines, 1961 saw the arrival at Newton Abbot brought forward to 11.17 am, and this was subsequently still further improved to 10.34 am before its long run was finally ended on 4 May 1968.

18 October 1985

After the floods

By 1960, when this picture was taken, most of the regular express passenger trains in the West Country were already diesel hauled, although in those early days failures were fairly frequent and it was not unusual to find a steam locomotive standing in for the regular 'Warship' Class diesel.

This was particularly so in the aftermath of the terrible flooding which occurred in October 1960, when the whole of the Exe valley became a moving lake, causing devastation in Tiverton, Exeter and many other places. Certain points on the GWR main line in Devon had always been vulnerable to flooding, in particular the crossing of the river Culm, just south of Hele & Bradninch station, and also just beyond Plympton on the outskirts of Plymouth. However, in steam days this did not present any real problems, unless the flow of water was sufficient to disturb the ballast, or the water level was more than about 12 inches above the rails. Providing speed was kept to walking pace, and the water was not so deep as to reach the fire, steam locomotives could plod on through flooded stretches of line without coming to any harm.

The new diesel locomotives were not so accommodating and were disinclined to get their feet wet, with the result that in October 1960 wholesale replacement of diesel by steam engines was made to keep the trains running over the flooded sections.

Things had still not returned to normal by Saturday 5 November 1960 when Newton Abbot-based No 5024 *Carew Castle* was hauling 'The Devonian' on the Paignton to Bristol section of its journey to Bradford, seen here passing the Devon General garage nearing the Lawes Bridge summit of the climb out of Torquay in fine style.

26 October 1985

Home from the hols

In the immediate post-war years the railways seemed to be slow to react to the vast increase in the number of people for whom full employment and the consequent paid holidays now became a reality. Each year the numbers going on holiday increased, and with so many tied to fixed works holiday periods, overcrowding on peak-period holiday trains became an accepted, if uncomfortable, part of the endurance test expected of any family seeking rest and recuperation by the sea.

Not that this was any change from what people had become accustomed to during the war years, when getting a seat on a train was regarded as sheer luxury, and sitting on one's kitbag in the corridor was normal. Sleeping on a night train, with one's feet in one carriage and head in another, sprawled across the lurching and very draughty corridor connection, cut off from the rest of the train by those heavy self-closing doors which were then a feature of any walk through the train, was an experience many will recall from those wartime night journeys.

Happily, the returning holidaymakers on 6 August 1949 will not have to endure these hardships, although they already appear to be fairly tightly packed in the corridors of the leading coaches of the 8.05 am Kingswear to Paddington train. 'County' Class 4-6-0 No 1023 *County of Oxford* has just restarted the train away from the stop at Torre station, and is making a noisy ascent past the Torre outer advanced starting signal and under Shiphay bridge.

It was not until 1952 that this train omitted stops at both Torre and Kingskerswell, having already called at all stations from Kingswear except Goodrington Sands Halt, which helped to account for the 5 hours exactly it was scheduled to take to reach Paddington. This was before the days of 'seat regulation' and fixed formation trains, and it is quite likely that the ten coaches out of Kingswear will be made up to 13 or 14 by the addition of further coaches to the rear of the train at Newton Abbot.

23 November 1985

Green issues

One of the less expected results of the Conservative 1953 Transport Act, with its devolution to the Regions of certain powers previously held by the Railway Executive, was the repainting in a modified GWR express livery of Western Region locomotives down to the smallest passenger tanks. The first visible evidence of this change of policy was seen in the spring of 1956, when two ex-GWR 2-6-0s selected for Royal Train duty on the Barnstaple branch were repainted in a rather more ornate version of the lined green livery previously reserved only for the principal express classes.

Initially the Railway Executive had ordained that the most powerful express class on each Region was to be painted in a lined light blue livery, and the ex-GWR 'King' Class were thus attired in the early 1950s. Those who had past experience of blue-painted steam locomotives predicted that the livery would be short-lived, as the blue pigment reacts unfavourably to the heat of a locomotive boiler, and so it proved.

During this period the mixed traffic classes were painted black, but lined out with red, cream and grey lines, in a close approximation to the livery of the pre-grouping London & North Western Railway, but without the many layers of varnish that gave the LNWR engines their attractive appearance when kept clean, as was normal in those days.

A less attractive feature of this livery on the ex-GWR engines was the red paint applied as a background to the brass name and number plates. As both the numbers and letters were raised above the backing plate, dirt tended to collect around them, and even when kept clean the plates were much more difficult to read than with the original black background. This is particularly noticeable in photographs of the period.

A few passenger tank engines acquired the lined black livery in the early 1950s but most were condemned to the unrelieved gloom of the all-black freight livery until 1957. Then the Western Region commenced painting *all* passenger engines green. And not just plain green either, but fully lined green, an adornment never carried by the smaller engines in later GWR days.

Our picture shows 2-6-2T No 5536, resplendent in the new livery, pulling away from Dunsford Halt on the Teign Valley line with the 10.43 am from Heathfield to Exeter on 1 March 1958.

30 November 1985

South Western rivals

Unlike the GWR, which was unique in maintaining its identity throughout its existence as an independent company, the London & South Western Railway had started life as the London & Southampton Railway. However, as early as 1839 it was realised that this title was inappropriate for a company which was beginning to look further West, although it was to be another 21 years before its first train reached Exeter.

The intervening years were spent in dispute over which route the line should take - whether to extend from Dorchester, across the undulating Dorset hills via Bridport, the so-called 'Coastal Route', or from Salisbury via Crewkerne and Axminster, known as the 'Central Route'. Just to confuse matters, the GWR and the Bristol & Exeter Railway would, at intervals, make their own proposals for a broad gauge connection across East Devon to the broad gauge route then being constructed from Westbury to Weymouth.

An independent company, the Salisbury & Yeovil, had meanwhile obtained an Act to build this part of the 'Central Route', and the LSWR eventually decided to support this and build the extension on to Exeter, arriving there in 1860. The monopoly of the broad gauge companies was now broken, much to the relief of the citizens of Exeter, who had never been much enamoured of the service provided by the Bristol & Exeter Railway.

Exeter's Queen Street station was not for long the terminus of the LSWR, which had already involved itself in the railway to North Devon, and was intent on reaching Plymouth and Cornwall. The station was rebuilt in 1933 and re-named Exeter Central, and my picture shows No 30676, an 0-4-4T of the 'M7' Class, designed by the redoubtable Dugald Drummond in 1897, leaving on a train of LSWR stock for Exmouth on 21 August 1954. As LSWR No 676, this engine came to Exeter when brand new for working semi-fast services on the main line. After an accident involving one of the class, they were mostly transferred to the London area, but No 676 was one of those which later returned to Exeter, where they were for many years the mainstay of the east Devon branches.

21 December 1985

'Prairie' from Kingsbridge

Ex-GWR 'Prairie' tank (2-6-2T) No 4561 chatters up out of the Avon valley towards Brent station, on the main line, with the 5.40 pm branch train from Kingsbridge on an early June evening in 1961. The fireman's work is done for this trip, so he leans back to study the embankment, with its rich profusion of grasses and wild flowers, all getting ready to make any hay fever sufferer's life a misery later in the month. The ivy-clad timber fenceposts lean defensively, in deference to decades of westerly gales.

The low evening sun throws the shadow of the locomotive on to the further bank, while the leaves of the background trees are turned back by a fresh north-westerly breeze. It appears to be a good evening for the gliding fraternity, as the cloud formations suggest there are plenty of 'thermals' about.

The Kingsbridge branch enjoyed a considerable parcels traffic, with over 60,000 items being handled each year. Most trains included at least one parcels van, and this one has two, both of Southern Railway design. They are marshalled next to the engine, ahead of the single passenger coach, to facilitate their transfer on to the rear of an eastbound passenger train at Brent.

The locomotive is one of the almost universally popular ex-Great Western branch line 2-6-2 tanks. With good power and capable of rapid acceleration, they were ideal engines for the hilly and often tortuous branch lines in Devon and Cornwall, where most of the early members of this class were stationed. The first batch were constructed at the GWR's Wolverhampton Works, at the rate of one a month from October 1906 to April 1908, at which time they were numbered in the 2161-2180 series. However, a general tidying up of GWR locomotive numbers in December 1912 saw the first batch re-numbered to 4500-4519, by which time the class had already been extended to 4529.

The subject of our picture, No 4561, was built in October 1924 and worked until May 1962, when she was withdrawn and sold to Woodham Bros at Barry for scrapping. Fortunately, like many other engines at Barry she was rescued for preservation, being acquired by the West Somerset Railway and taken to Minehead, where she is now back in service.

11 January 1986

Off to Kingswear

Twenty years before the Dart Valley Light Railway Company Ltd appeared on this scene, a local train from Exeter to Kingswear pulls out of Paignton station towards the then very busy Sands Road level crossing. It is Saturday 6 September 1952 and carriage sidings then occupied the site which was later to become the headquarters, workshops and station for the preserved Torbay & Dartmouth Railway.

During the week in the summer these sidings would be occupied with carriages detached from trains arriving at Paignton from London, Manchester, South Wales and the Midlands, some in order to lighten the load before tackling the climb up to Churston, and others regularly terminating at Paignton. The normal maximum load for a 'Castle' Class locomotive proceeding to Kingswear would be ten coaches, with proportionately fewer for the less powerful engines.

Many of the carriages detached at Paignton were regular workings, and in those days, except for certain London trains, those coming from beyond Bristol would be unlikely to make more than one journey in the day. The stock was worked in accordance with the 'coach working programme' to ensure that each day the correct number and formation of coaches were ready to work each scheduled train. Weekly amendments to the 'programme' covered special arrangements for parties and all the day-to-day variations needed to cope with varying passenger loadings. Although these daily alterations to the basic pattern were committed to the printed page, in practice considerable local initiative had to be exercised in order to ensure that coaches required to strengthen outgoing trains, especially on summer Saturdays, were in fact on the spot when required. Canny local stock controllers would therefore 'acquire' coaches during the week, to provide themselves with enough stock to ensure passengers were all accommodated on their return journey.

As this picture was taken late on a Saturday morning the sidings are relatively empty as 'Star' Class 4-6-0 No 4034 *Queen Adelaide* leaves for Kingswear. The empty train reporting number frame on her smokebox indicates that she is to work an up express later in the day, after being turned on the Kingswear turntable. Sure enough, she returned on the 1.40 pm express from Kingswear to Paddington, and worked right through to London.

This could well have been her last express working, as the records show that she was withdrawn from service in September 1952 after no less than 42 years in main-line service.

Rolling-stock operation today is vastly different from the 1950s; the flexibility of those times has been completely lost in the drive for increased mileage from each vehicle, and mileages which would then have been respectable for a week are now achieved daily, week in week out.

25 January 1986

Called up

In both World Wars full advantage was taken of the ability of standard British railway locomotives to run on the mainland of Europe, with only slight modifications being needed. Although the main type selected for overseas war service in the First World War came from the Great Central Railway, and over 500 Robinson-designed 2-8-0s were built for home and overseas service, many Great Western Railway engines were also taken over by the War Department for the use of their Railway Operating Division. This was then a most important arm of the military, before the era of reliable heavy road transport, other than horses and mules, and provided most of the transport for supplies from the French Channel ports to the front line.

In 1917 no fewer than 62 GWR Dean 0-6-0 goods engines were 'called up' by the War Department, and most were sent to France. However, some had a much more adventurous journey to make and ended up in Greece, at Salonika, which was then a base for our troops who were fighting the Turks in the mountains to the north. At Salonika they were joined by some even more elderly GWR 0-6-0s, Armstrong goods engines built in the 1870s, which were shipped out from England in two batches of eight. Unfortunately one of the ships carrying these engines was sunk in the English Channel on its way out, and eight Armstrong goods engines are still lying out there, waiting to be discovered - a job for the sub-aqua division of the Torbay & Dartmouth Railway volunteers, perhaps?

After performing their war service in the Balkans, most of these engines were eventually returned to the GWR, though some not until 1921. The Dean goods engines being repaired and returned to traffic, but the Armstrongs were by then worn out and were scrapped. A few of both classes were retained by the local operators and were absorbed into the Ottoman Railway. This later became part of the Turkish State Railways, and at least one of the Dean goods engines crossed to Asian Turkey and ended its days at Izmir, where it was finally cut up in the late 1950s.

The largest GWR engines taken for war service in 1917 were 11 of the standard Churchward 2-6-0s then being built at Swindon, which went straight over to France. Only one of the Churchward 2-6-0s has been preserved, No 5322, one of the 11 that went to France, and this engine can now be seen among the Great Western Society's collection at Didcot.

Sister engine No 6385, one of the first two 'Moguls' (2-6-0s) to be painted in the BR lined green livery for working the Royal Train to Barnstaple in May 1956 (see also pages 16 and 178), is seen pulling away from Kingskerswell with the 8.06 am from Sheffield to Kingswear on Saturday 25 August of that year.

8 February 1986

Moretonhampstead

The branch terminus at Moretonhampstead on 26 January 1952, with 2-6-2 tank No 4547, itself half hidden by steam, supplying plenty of steam heat to the two auto-trailers to warm the passengers on this cheerless morning. A moderate fall of snow overnight has not been sufficient to delay the train service, but would no doubt have made the road to Newton Abbot hazardous, in the days when pre-snowfall salting of the roads was unknown, and subsequent treatment usually confined only to the more difficult stretches. The railway could then be a lifeline for those communities fortunate enough to have stations or halts within easy walking distance.

The inhabitants of Moretonhampstead originally gained their rail connection to Newton Abbot, opened in July 1866, more from the desire of the broad gauge South Devon Railway, backed by the GWR, to counter the intentions of the 'narrow' (standard) gauge London & South Western Railway, than from any direct wish to serve the local villages.

A scheme had been presented to Parliament in 1861 for a narrow gauge 'Devon Central' line connecting Exeter with Moretonhampstead, Chagford, Okehampton and Lydford, but this was defeated. The broad gauge companies, fearing the competition from a narrow gauge line crossing territory they regarded as their own, returned the following year with proposals for broad gauge branches to Launceston and Moretonhampstead, both of which were successful.

It took four years to complete the Moretonhampstead & South Devon Railway which, when opened, had stations at Bovey, Lustleigh and Moretonhampstead. Teigngrace was added in 1867 and Chudleigh Road (later re-named Heathfield) in 1874. Although providing access to Dartmoor for generations of people in the Torbay area, the line itself did not climb on to the moor and only reached a height of 550 feet at its terminus.

In contrast, on the other side of the moor, the Princetown branch climbed to 1,395 feet and was consequently much more vulnerable at times of heavy snowfall. During the famous blizzard of 9 March 1891, the evening train from Princetown was marooned in a snow-filled cutting and the six passengers and three train crew had to spend a bitter night on the moor before being found by railwaymen who had fought their way up from Dousland on foot. Even then the passengers elected to stay on the train, and spent another night there before being taken to a nearby farmhouse the following morning. It was not until 17 March that the line was eventually cleared through to Yelverton and a further day before the top end could be cleared to Princetown.

15 February 1986

Summer Saturdays

Summer in the West Country is the time when everything comes alive again. Today it is the motorways which carry most of the visitors to the South West, but in the post-war period it was the railways that bore this burden. The woefully inadequate main roads of that time, barely improved since the 1930s, were quite unable to cope with the rising tide of weekend travellers, and the railway each summer carried an ever-increasing flow of holidaymakers, which eventually peaked towards the end of the 1950s.

Every year this flow became a torrent in the last weekend of July, when the start of the industrial holiday fortnight in the Midlands coincided with the first weekend of the school summer holidays. To cope with this rush many extra relief trains had to be run, and year by year the number gradually increased to the point where the timetable planners were unable to find 'paths' for any further trains during the hours of the day that most people wished to travel.

By 1955, on this peak Saturday, there were already 40 trains scheduled to pass through Newton Abbot, bound for Penzance, Newquay or Paignton, between 1.20 am and 7.10 am, roughly one train every 9 minutes.

The first of these to set out on its long journey was the 3.57 pm on Friday from Newcastle to Penzance, which was due through Newton Abbot at 1.45 am. By that time there were already three trains ahead of it, all reliefs to Cornwall, from Birmingham (Moor St), Coventry and Sheffield. Behind it was the first overnight relief from Paddington to Penzance, closely followed by the first relief train from Birmingham (Moor Street) to Torquay and Paignton, which was due to disgorge its load of snoozy but expectant passengers on to the Torquay platform at 2.37 am. Before 6.00 am, a further 13 trains would have arrived at Torquay, all going forward to Paignton, and one to Kingswear.

That is, of course, if all were running to time, but on this peak weekend that was the last thing to expect. Between the neat graphs of the timetable planners and the live steam trains out on the rails, drivers straining to pick up the glimmer of the oil-lit signal lamps, firemen coaxing reluctant fires into renewed life, and signalmen passing each train from box to box, there existed a gulf which at times resembled a chasm. Things did not often go according to plan on that night.

Here we see a typical summer Saturday train headed by a BR Standard 2-10-0 freight locomotive, No 92218, pressed into passenger service on the 9.55 am Swansea to Kingswear train, in Torquay station on 3 September 1960. On the centre road is 2-6-2 tank No 6146, waiting to provide rear-end banking assistance to up trains on the climb to Torre.

22 February 1986

Torre banker

The picture of Torquay station on the previous page included the engine provided on summer Saturdays for assisting passenger trains up the 1 in 55 climb to Torre, standing in the centre road between duties. Here we see a banker in action, as 2-6-2 tank No 5533 pushes the 8.52 am Paignton to Leeds train, hauled by 4-6-0 No 6997 *Bryn-Ivor Hall*, through Torre station at 9.16 am on Saturday 9 August 1958. No 5533 looks a little odd, as she is blowing off furiously and the steam escaping from the safety valves is hiding her chimney from view.

Rear-end assistance, or 'banking' as it is usually known, is more often associated with the old-fashioned loose-coupled freight trains, where an engine at the rear was necessary on heavy gradients to avoid a broken coupling allowing the rear of the train to run back down the hill out of control.

With passenger trains, the continuous vacuum brakes meant that there was no danger of the rear end running back, in the unlikely event of a screw coupling failure, so that if extra power was needed it was usually provided at the front end. However, in certain specific locations banking of passenger trains was allowed, where this would enable an engine powerful enough to haul, say, 13 coaches over the remainder of the line to London or Bristol to surmount a short continuous gradient which would otherwise restrict it to nine coaches. Such a gradient was the 1 in 55 climb from the platform end at Torquay up to Torre.

Banking in these circumstances was governed by strict regulations, which called for the banking engine to be coupled to the rear of the train as far as Torre, if the train was to stop there. Otherwise the banking engine would simple buffer up to the back of the up train while the passengers were boarding in Torquay station.

When the guard gave the 'right away', the train engine would give a double 'cock crow' on its whistle, to which the banker would reply in like manner. Both engines were then ready to proceed, and with another pip on the whistle the train driver would open his regulator while the banker driver did the same, moving the train steadily out of the platform and up the hill to Torre. The banker was allowed only to proceed as far as the Torre up outer advanced starting signal, which stood just short of Shiphay bridge (see page 14). Here the banker driver would close his regulator and drop away from the rear of the train, stopping short of the signal. On receiving permission from the Torre signalman he would then return down the up line, crossing over to the down line opposite Torre goods shed, and so back to Torquay to await the next up train needing assistance. On summer Saturday mornings two engines would be required for banking duties at Torquay, and often locomotives recently ex-shops from the Newton Abbot Locomotive Works would be used.

The train seen entering the down platform at Torre, hauled by 4-6-0s Nos 6852 *Headbourne Grange*, tender first, and 5949 *Trematon Hall*, is probably the overnight service from Hull to Paignton.

1 March 1986

'Bulldogs'

Until the abolition of the broad gauge in 1892, the GWR had always regarded its 'narrow' gauge engines as of secondary importance; very few of them were given names, for instance, and standing alongside the broad gauge leviathans, most narrow gauge engines looked distinctly puny. After 1892, with the broad gauge finally interred, the GWR Locomotive Department, under William Dean and his assistant George Jackson Churchward, set about providing the company with the locomotives and rolling-stock necessary to carry an increasing volume of traffic.

First came the supremely beautiful 4-2-2 'Achilles' Class 7 foot 8 inch 'Singles'. It was the received wisdom of that period to build inside cylinder single wheelers for express trains, and most of the large railway companies did so. But their days were numbered. The provision of corridors and restaurant cars in the principal expresses meant that within ten years the loads were too much for the adhesion of a single driving wheel, and these graceful machines were relegated to less onerous duties.

West of Newton Abbot something stronger was needed urgently, and in 1895 the 'Duke of Cornwall' Class appeared. These were 5 foot 8 inch 4-4-0s, similar in outline to the 'Achilles' Class but without their raised-top firebox and with an extended smokebox. They were intended for use in the West Country and bore suitable names, one of which being *Tor Bay*.

Four years later one of the 'Duke of Cornwall' Class, No 3352 *Camel*, was turned out from Swindon Works bearing one of Mr Churchward's new standard domeless boilers, and thus was born what was later to become known as the 'Bulldog' Class, although these early examples did not acquire the familiar domeless tapered boiler until 1906. The 'Bulldogs' were to become part of the West Country scene for the next 42 years. From initially working only the principal express trains to Penzance, as further members of the class were built they spread their activities to semi-fast passenger trains all over the GWR system. Withdrawals started in 1929 and continued up to the outbreak of war in 1939, when two were reinstated; one of these was No 3335, a familiar engine locally.

During the 1930s and 1940s 'Bulldogs' were in daily use on local passenger trains between Exeter and Kingswear, but their main use at that time was for piloting the 'Kings' and 'Castles' over the South Devon banks between Newton Abbot and Plymouth.

Here we see 'Bulldog' No 3407 *Madras* doing a little light shunting at the west end of Newton Abbot station on 1 July 1948, towards the end of her long life which lasted from April 1904 to December 1949.

5 April 1986

Royal Albert Bridge (1)

Isambard Kingdom Brunel's finest architectural achievement, the Royal Albert Bridge across the Tamar between St Budeaux and Saltash, was floodlit during the summer of its centenary year, 1959.

We owe a debt to the Parliament of 1845 for turning down the original proposal in the Cornwall Railway Bill of that year, which included not only an unduly severely graded and tortuous route, but a crossing of the river Tamar by steam train ferry to Torpoint, adjacent to the already existing steam road ferry. Doubtless the company were seeking to conserve their capital and baulked at the cost which a bridge would involve. Fortunately the House of Lords Committee thought otherwise and suggested that the company return with a better route and, if possible, avoidance of the river ferry.

It was at this point that the Cornwall Railway turned to I. K. Brunel, who was already Engineer to the Great Western and South Devon railways, for a new survey of their route from Plymouth to Truro and Falmouth. He proposed that on leaving Plymouth the line should proceed to St Budeaux, crossing the Tamar river by a high-level bridge to Saltash, thereafter regaining roughly the route originally planned though with improved alignment and gradients.

In this form the Cornwall Railway Bill received the Royal Assent in 1846 and work could now proceed, subject to Admiralty approval for the bridge design. Several of Brunel's proposals were turned down, before final approval was granted for the building of the bridge we know today. One option rejected by Brunel at an early stage was for a single span of 850 feet, which even he decided, perhaps wisely, might be too much for the materials of the day.

He settled eventually for two main spans, each 455 feet in length and 100 feet above high water, with seven approach spans on the Devon side and ten leading into Saltash. Even this was greater than anything previously attempted, and with the materials available at that time demanded a design which is still unique, and was a development of his bridge over the River Wye at Chepstow for the Great Western Railway.

One of the major problems was to find a footing for the central pier, which consists of four octagonal cast iron columns on a masonry base. At high tide here the water is 80 feet deep and Brunel needed all the experience gained in working on the Chepstow bridge and on his father's Thames Tunnel to design a 300-ton iron cylinder to act both as a compressed air diving bell and coffer dam, inside which the work could be completed.

Each of the main spans is a combined arch and suspension bridge. Massive chains, part of which were originally made for the Clifton suspension bridge, are attached to either end of a huge elliptical tube constructed from wrought iron plates strengthened internally. The platform on which the trains run is supported from both, the whole being cross-braced into a very rigid structure. Each span was constructed on site on the Devon side and floated out into the river on pontoons, before being raised by hydraulic jacks at the rate of six feet per week, while the supporting piers were being built.

Ill health prevented Brunel from attending the opening by HRH Prince Albert on 2 May 1859, but he was later that month to see his completed masterpiece from a couch propelled across the bridge on an open truck, before his premature death in September 1859.

3 May 1986

'Merchant Navy' at Dainton

The rare sight of a Southern Region rebuilt 'Merchant Navy' Class 'Pacific' breasting the summit of the bank has brought the Dainton Sidings signalman to the window of his box to have a closer look. Although Mr O. V. S. Bulleid's lightweight 'Pacifics' were regular performers over the South Devon banks on the post-war exchange workings, his 'Merchant Navy' locomotives were very infrequent visitors to this area, and did not normally work beyond Exeter Central on the express trains from London Waterloo, although they did make occasional visits to Newton Abbot for weighing, after repairs at Exmouth Junction shed.

This particular train on 20 September 1958 is a special sponsored by the magazine *Trains Illustrated* and includes three Pullman cars in its gross load of 334 tons. No 35023 *Holland Afrika Line* has worked the train up from Plymouth in the hands of Driver Gidley from Exmouth Junction shed. Earlier in the run he had been in trouble on Hemerdon bank, the long climb out of Plympton, which was passed at 56 mph. Apparently when attempting to open the regulator for the climb ahead, Driver Gidley had been unable to lift it beyond a certain point, and by the time he called his mate over to help, speed had dropped to 14 mph. With the regulator well open, and the three-cylinder beat echoing back from the trees, *Holland Afrika Line* soon recovered to 20 mph, despite the 1 in 42 adverse gradient.

On Dainton bank, now 4 minutes ahead of schedule, no great effort appears to have been made, as the speed over the summit was recorded by an observer on the train as only 18 mph.

By the time this picture was taken all the 'Merchant Navy' Class had been rebuilt to a more conventional locomotive outline, but when they first appeared from Eastleigh Works in the early months of 1941 they created a minor sensation. Described as mixed traffic engines, that is to handle freight as well as passenger trains, with their 'air-smoothed' casing they more resembled streamlined express passenger locomotives, which was in fact what they were.

To produce a new class of express passenger engine in the middle of the worst year of the war was remarkable enough, but also to pack into it a number of novel design features, new at least to the Southern Railway, was typical of their designer, O. V. S. Bulleid. He only became the Chief Mechanical Engineer of the Southern Railway in 1937, having previously been an Assistant to Sir Nigel Gresley on the London & North Eastern Railway, and intended to have his place in locomotive history.

This he certainly achieved with the original 'Merchant Navy' 4-6-2s, with their unusual oilbath-enclosed and chain-driven valve gear, distinctive wheels, 280 lb per square inch boiler pressure and air-smoothed casing. Even the numbers were different from anything previously seen - the first was No 21C1 *Channel Packet*.

Although they had the usual 'Pacific' tendency to slip on starting, and I can remember observing some quite horrendous and almost uncontrollable slipping from these engines leaving Exeter Central on heavily loaded wartime trains, they put up some remarkable performances over the years, and were thought by many to be even better after rebuilding.

17 May 1986

Calstock viaduct

Although the Royal Albert Bridge at Saltash is the most famous rail crossing from Devon into Cornwall, another less well-known rail crossing of the river Tamar still exists a few miles further north at Calstock.

This imposing viaduct was built by the Plymouth, Devonport & South Western Junction Railway and completed in 1908, in the course of upgrading the East Cornwall Mineral Railway and connecting at Bere Alston to the main line operated by the London & South Western Railway between Exeter and Plymouth.

The original mineral railway was built to carry the products of, and supplies for, the many mines and quarries in the Kit Hill and Gunnislake area. Opened in 1872, and built to a gauge of 3 feet 6 inches, it ran 7¹/₂ miles from Kelly Bray, near Callington, through Gunnislake to the riverside quays in Calstock, reached by means of a rope-worked incline on a gradient of roughly 1 in 6.

Calstock was then a busy river port, with sea-going schooners and barges brought up the river by steam paddle tugs. These vessels would bring coal and timber for use in the mines, returning with tin, copper and arsenic from the mines, and granite from the quarries.

During the 36 years that the East Cornwall Mineral Railway was operating, its traffic, up to 70,000 tons a year, was worked by two 0-4-0 saddle tanks built by Nielsons of Glasgow in 1871. They were housed in a shed at the top of the incline, which can still be seen today, and worked the traffic onwards to Kelly Bray. One of them survived until 1927, rebuilt and regauged, as 0-4-2ST *Hesperus* on Colonel Stephens's Selsey Tramway.

In 1898 the Plymouth, Devonport & South Western Junction Railway, which already owned the mineral railway, and had opened its own line from Lydford through Bere Alston to Devonport in 1890, was spurred into further activity by the possibility of a light railway being constructed from the GWR station at Saltash to Callington. With the help of the London & South Western Railway, which was already operating the PD&SWJR's main line, the latter obtained the Bere Alston & Calstock Light Railway Order, enabling it to extend the East Cornwall Mineral Railway across a viaduct at Calstock and thence up to Bere Alston, still on the 3 ft 6 in gauge, but now authorised to carry passengers. However, before construction commenced a further Order was obtained changing the gauge to the standard 4 ft 8¹/₂ in.

To work the new railway, three new engines were ordered, an 0-6-0 side tank and two rather imposing 0-6-2 side tanks, all from locomotive manufacturers Hawthorn Leslie and named respectively *A. S. Harris*, *Earl of Mount Edgcumbe* and *Lord St Levan*. These engines continued to work the line until 1952, assisted after 1923 by Southern Railway '02' Class 0-4-4Ts and other more unlikely engines, such as an 'X2' Class 4-4-0 which ventured on to the line in 1926 with a six-coach special. A more unsuitable engine for this sharply curved and graded line could hardly be imagined, and the experiment was not repeated.

The '02s' continued to work the line until 1961, and No 30225 is here seen crossing the viaduct on 15 April 1961 with the 4.23 pm from Callington. They were gradually replaced by Ivatt 2-6-2Ts until the diesels took over, and today, although the line is open only as far as Gunnislake, it is still well worth a visit, having been saved from complete closure by the alternative circuitous road link to Plymouth.

24 May 1986

'Greyhounds'

On page 36 we saw 'Merchant Navy' Class 'Pacific' No 35023 *Holland Afrika Line* passing Dainton Sidings signal box with a special passenger train. This was a rare enough event for one day, but better was to follow, as the next normal service stopping train, the 4.32 pm from Plymouth to Exeter, was double-headed by two ex-London & South Western Railway 'T9' Class 4-4-0s. They are seen passing under the bridge carrying the main Totnes to Newton Abbot road over the railway line, as the train snakes its way up the increasingly severe gradients to the summit at Dainton tunnel. The leading engine, No 30712, now on ex-Great Western Railway metals, should be showing a solitary white disc or lamp in front of the chimney to indicate a stopping passenger train, but is still carrying the two white discs from its previous duty; this was the Southern Railway route indication for a London Waterloo to Plymouth train, as these two 4-4-0s had brought the special down to Plymouth and were now using the up stopper, normally hauled by one of the Bulleid 'West Country' Class 'Pacifics', as a means of usefully returning to their home depot at Exmouth Junction, on the eastern outskirts of Exeter.

The 'T9s' were the most popular and long-lived of the several 4-4-0 express classes designed for the LSWR by their Chief Mechanical Engineer Dugald Drummond. Coming to the LSWR in 1895, after an earlier career with the Caledonian Railway, this rugged Scotsman was responsible for several successful classes of 4-4-0, though his attempts with a four-cylinder 4-4-0 with unconnected driving wheels and later 4-6-0 classes were less than satisfactory.

The 'T9s' on this train, still carrying their LSWR numbers 712 and 726, plus the 30000 added by British Railways, were both in the first batch of 30 ordered from Dubs and Co of Glasgow at a cost of £3,200 for each engine and tender. The order was placed in March 1898 for delivery by the end of 1899, and although five were delayed by a strike at the works, our two arrived during 1899.

As might be expected, their appearance then was slightly different from the sleek but somewhat austere aspect they had in later years, after superheating had extended their smoke-boxes. The early engines had smokebox wingplates, sandboxes included in the leading splashers, and a shapely cast chimney, but the effect was rather spoilt by the rectangular box enclosing the firebox watertubes, which extended forward from the cab between the driving wheel splashers.

In all, 66 of the class were built, and although it was not until they were fitted with superheated boilers in the 1920s that their true potential was realised, they had already been given the nickname 'Greyhounds' for their performance on the fairly lightweight trains on which they were mainly used during their first 20 years.

No 726, the second engine here, was one of several which lost its large bogie tender in 1928, when it was transferred to the Central Section of the Southern Railway to operate out of Brighton. It retained its six-wheeled tender to the end, which came at Ashford in August 1959. No 712 had by then already been withdrawn, as it lasted only another two months from the date of this picture, being broken up at Brighton in November 1958. Happily, one of the class has been preserved in working order as part of the National Collection.

21 June 1986

Rule 'Britannia'?

The first of the British Railways Standard locomotive designs, the 'Britannia' Class '7' mixed traffic 4-6-2, was introduced in 1951, the year of the Festival of Britain. The initial batch of locomotives were allocated to the Eastern Region for use on the old Great Eastern section, where they were an immediate success and revolutionised the services between Liverpool Street and Norwich, taking over from the somewhat rough-riding 'B17' 4-6-0s, the first of which were by then over 20 years old.

The next batch, mostly carrying names from old broad gauge engines, came to the Western Region, where locally they went down like the proverbial lead balloon, being about as popular as clinker on the firegrate. However, strangely enough those that went to South Wales were well liked by the Cardiff Canton crews, who used them with great success on the principal expresses to London, such as the 'Capitals United' and 'Red Dragon'.

In the West Country, and especially at Newton Abbot, where No 70022 Tornado was based, they were regarded with great suspicion, and not without reason. The cab layout was entirely different from that of the Great Western in which some crews had spent a lifetime. Being left-hand-drive engines, the driver's and fireman's positions were reversed. The regulator was not as sensitive as the Great Western pattern and the 'Britannias' had the tendency of all 'Pacifics' to slip on starting, which was never a problem with the sure-footed 'Kings' and 'Castles'.

In addition, the handrails attached to the outside of the smoke deflectors proved to be a hazard as they partially obstructed the driver's view of the signals, already made difficult because the signal positions on the Great Western were all arranged for a right-hand driving position. This problem surfaced following the most serious accident to befall a 'Britannia' when, approaching Didcot, the driver claimed he was unsighted by the handrail and consequently failed to slow down for a diversion on to the slow line. As a result the locomotive overturned.

Local opinion in Newton Abbot at the time put this down to the relatively high setting of the boiler, giving the 'Britannias' a higher centre of gravity than the 'Kings' and 'Castles', and consequently a greater tendency to roll over in the circumstances of this accident. A 'King' or a 'Castle' would have stayed on its wheels, they said, a statement that must remain for ever not proven. The offending handrails were later removed from the Western Region 'Britannias', being replaced by a series of handholds cut out of the deflectors.

By early 1957 the 'Britannias' had been withdrawn from West Country depots and concentrated at Cardiff, where they were appreciated, being exchanged for 'Castle' Class 4-6-0s, which were both popular with the local crews and more suited to the local terrain. Thereafter, the Cardiff 'Britannias' were only occasional visitors to the South West.

Taken in September 1956, just before this exchange took place, our picture is of No 70016 Ariel leaving Newton Abbot with the 7.30 am from Penzance to Manchester. The mixed rake of ex-LMSR and ex-GWR coaches is in the carmine and cream livery of the early 1950s; the train has passed Hackney yard and come under the bridge leading to the Passage House Inn, and is now alongside the Teign estuary. Passing in the down direction is a mercifully short freight hauled by 4-6-0 No 5934 Kneller Hall.

26 July 1986

The versatile '45s'

Backed by the tall pine trees which dominated the station and separated the railway from the banks of the river Avon, ex-GWR 2-6-2 tank No 4561 pulls rapidly away from Avonwick station for Gara Bridge, the next stop on its way from Brent to Kingsbridge on 1 August 1960. The clean white exhaust steam, having done its work in the cylinders, now arches over the two-coach train before being dispersed by the breeze and the warm sunshine.

On this slightly falling gradient, as the line twists and turns with the river Avon, the engine's exhaust beats will soon merge, and the rattle of the train wheels on the jointed track will gradually be submerged in the buzz of eager insects investigating the roadside verge. Would you believe this peaceful scene was taken on what was then August Bank Holiday Monday? It was.

The versatile '45s' were ideal engines for branch-line work, equally at home on passenger or freight duties, very free running, and with a good turn of speed. Capable of 60 mph without the need for either downgrade or following wind, they could also haul a good load when needed. Today No 4555 demonstrates this well when taking a packed seven-coach Torbay & Dartmouth Railway train over the 'gable' between Goodrington and Kingswear, which at its steepest is 1 in 60 on the approach to Churston from the Paignton direction.

The '45s' were one of the standard classes designed by the GWR's renowned Chief Mechanical Engineer, George Jackson Churchward, who came from Stoke Gabriel in Devon and started his career with the South Devon Railway in 1873 as a pupil, at Newton Abbot, of Mr John Wright, that company's Locomotive Superintendent. The South Devon Railway was absorbed by the GWR in 1876, and by 1896 Churchward had risen to Works Manager at Swindon, eventually becoming Locomotive Superintendent in 1902.

By this time he had already developed his ideas on the standard classes which would be necessary to provide the GWR with a stock of locomotives capable of meeting the Operating Department's requirements for the next 20 years - and, as it turned out, for much longer than that.

For the branch lines two classes of 2-6-2T were envisaged and the first to appear was the prototype of the smaller-wheeled (4 ft 1½ in) class. The prototype engine, No 115, built at Swindon in 1904, later became No 4400 under the 1912 renumbering scheme. Although ten further engines of this class were built during the following year, it was evidently felt that despite their terrific powers of acceleration, a larger driving wheel would be generally more useful, especially on the longer branch lines, or where some main-line work would be required.

Consequently, a 4ft 7½ in version emerged from the GWR's Wolverhampton Works in 1906, the last new engines to be constructed there. These were numbered 2161 to 2180 when built, but later became 4500 to 4519. As built they had a short smokebox and a bunker no higher than the level of the side tanks. The bunker was later extended upwards and outwards and the smokebox lengthened, but apart from detail modifications and a variety of chimney patterns over the years, those that lasted until the end of the steam era were still very much as originally built during the period 1906 to 1924. During this time 75 of the class had been built. A further 100 engines were constructed between 1927 and 1929, but these can be identified by their larger-capacity sloping side tanks.

2 August 1986

Full house at Newton Abbot

In contrast to the peaceful scene at Avonwick, this picture shows a very busy Newton Abbot on 28 July 1951, which was so typical of the peak summer Saturdays through the 1950s.

This was the peak Saturday of those days for down trains, when all the Midland factories closed down for a fortnight at the commencement of the school holidays. The pressure on the railways was immense, and every effort was made to carry all those who wished to travel, to the extent that some overnight trains from Wolverhampton arrived in four parts, and many others were duplicated.

To say that Newton Abbot was in those days a scene of intense activity during the peak summer Saturdays would be understating the case. Almost all the Saturday trains to Plymouth and Cornwall needed an assistant engine to get them safely over the South Devon hills, and consequently most of these trains, even though shown as non-stop in the public timetables, had in fact to stop to attach a pilot engine. Most down Paignton and Kingswear trains also stopped, either to provide connections for the passengers, or to enable engines or crews to be changed.

Needless to say, keeping this flow of trains moving needed a considerable team effort by the staff, who had to deal with down trains arriving on average every 9 minutes that day between 9.30 am and 4.00 pm. Consequently there was hardly a moment during the day when there was not at least one train in the station, and occasionally all six running roads could be occupied.

This picture was taken at 4.07 pm, with at least four of the six roads in use. Just leaving on the down through road are 4-6-0s Nos 6001 *King Edward VII* piloting 5090 *Neath Abbey* on the second part of the down 'Cornish Riviera Express'. The 'King' is carrying the alloy headboard and train number applicable to the main train, which it had brought from Paddington to Newton Abbot, and on which it had been replaced by two fresh engines which have already departed on their non-stop run to Truro. On the occasions that a 'King' was provided for both parts of the 'Cornish Riviera', this produced the only working of double-headed 'Kings' which was normally seen.

Next to this train on the down relief platform road, and causing havoc to the timetable, is a left-over from the night trains, 2-8-0 No 3800 on a parcels train, probably the 10.18 pm from Paddington, due into Newton at 5.33 am. After spending 38 minutes occupying one of the two available down platforms, it was eventually terminated and removed to the carriage sidings.

Next left, on the down main platform road, and taking water, is 4-6-0 No 6973 *Bricklehampton Hall* which had arrived 5 minutes earlier with the 10.40 am Paddington to Kingswear. She was 104 minutes late, which was not too bad considering that the day trains had started with a 66-minute late arrival, and since 9.25 am there had been 43 down trains, only two of which had run through non-stop.

Finally, standing outside Newton Abbot West signal box on the up relief platform road, is 'Star' Class 4-6-0 No 4059 *Princess Patricia*, just arrived back from Paignton after working the 6.55 am from Wolverhampton, and now anxiously waiting to get across to the shed as soon as a path is available.

This was to be last summer that the Churchward 'Star' and 'Saint' 4-6-0s appeared at Newton Abbot in any number. Eight 'Stars' and two 'Saints' were seen working that day, out of a total tally of 155 different engines.

9 August 1986

Liskeard & Caradon

Almost in the shadow of the magnificent Moorswater viaduct (see also page 72), which carries the main line to Penzance across the valley of the East Looe river, this little shed at Moorswater was home to two of the ex-GWR '45xx' and '55xx' Class 2-6-2 tanks. During the week one engine would work the passenger service, while the other hauled the daily freight train. On summer Saturdays both engines would be used on passenger trains, frequently abandoning the timetable and shuttling to and fro between Liskeard and Looe, connecting with as many of the late-running main-line trains as possible.

The shed was originally built in about 1861 to house the engines of the two railways which then made an end-on junction at this point - the Liskeard & Looe Railway and the Liskeard & Caradon Railway. It was enlarged in 1878, and by 1909, when the GWR took over the working of both lines, included a carriage shop 100 feet long and a blacksmith's shop, which lay to the left of the water tank and had been roofless for many years before this picture was taken on 15 March 1960.

The line which disappears behind the shed building was, until closed in 1917, the main and only line of the Liskeard & Caradon Railway. Built in 1846, and originally intended to carry lime and coal inland and to tap the granite resources of the Cheesewring area beyond Caradon Hill, copper ore soon became its principal traffic from the rich lodes then being developed in the South Caradon area.

The railway was worked on the horse and gravity principle. Hired horses - the railway could not afford its own - hauled the wagons up the line in the morning. Then, in the late afternoon, when the wagons had all been loaded, each was despatched down the line on its own, with a brakeman in command equipped with a whistle to warn of his approach at level crossings. No doubt there was plenty of competition for the job of brakeman on the Liskeard & Caradon Railway among the local youth.

During these early years, and this was well before the Cornwall Railway, opened in 1859, had been built, all the traffic from the Liskeard & Caradon Railway had to be transhipped into barges for onward travel down the Liskeard & Looe Union Canal to Looe, where it would again be transhipped into coastal craft. The limestone came from the Plymouth area, and the coal and copper ore traffic was with South Wales. By 1860 the traffic had become too much for both the horses and the canal, so the Liskeard & Looe Union Canal Company built a railway from Moorswater to Looe, alongside their canal. At the same time the Liskeard & Caradon changed to steam power, and from 1862 a Joint Committee of the two companies operated both lines as one.

It was another 42 years before a connection was eventually built to the main line, by which time this had been taken over by the GWR. Because of the difference in height between Moorswater and the main line, this new extension was both steep and tortuous, and on the opening day the last train, hauled by 0-6-0 tank *Looe*, which had been purchased specially for the new extension, stalled on the climb back up to Liskeard. This would have stranded the many Plymouth passengers in Liskeard had not the manager of the Liskeard & Looe Railway paid the GWR to put on a special train to get them home.

16 August 1986

Getting the picture

Fisherman are said to excel at describing the ones that got away, but railway photographers could run them pretty close. All have tales to tell of the superb shots they would have had, but for that little patch of cloud which appeared as the train approached, only to disperse again before the last coach had passed, or of the train that came the other way at the wrong moment - not to mention the ever-present hazard that double exposures presented in the days of the folding bellows camera. And before the advent of the single lens reflex camera, shooting one's picture with the lens cap still in position was not unknown.

With today's focal plane shuttered SLR equipment, provided you follow the instructions it has almost become difficult not to get a reasonable result. The quality of both cameras and films having improved so enormously over the last 30 years, today the photographer can concentrate on the content and composition of his picture, confident that the camera and film will deliver a technically correct record.

One of the problems with the folding cameras of earlier years was that if you were not very careful when handling them, they would soon get out of alignment, throwing one side of the picture out of focus. But worse than this for the railway photographer was the universal use of between-lens Compur-type shutters on almost all the cameras that came within most people's price range. Although these might be marked for 1/250th or 1/500th of a second exposure, these markings referred more to the amount of light reaching the film than to the actual stopping power of the shutter, when dealing with an object moving at 60 mph such as an express train. Even during an exposure of 1/500th of a second, a speeding train will move several inches while the shutter is open, and with a between-lens shutter acceptable sharpness of the front end of the train is not attainable, unless it is given some assistance.

This can take the form of a slight pan of the camera along the line of movement of the train, so reducing the degree of train movement relative to the camera. If well executed, this will increase the sharpness of the front of the train to an acceptable level, without impairing the sharpness of the rest of the picture to any noticeable degree. The difficulty comes in panning down the correct line, gradually increasing the movement of the camera as the train approaches, and then pressing the shutter release at the right moment. It is at this point that you realise that the sun, which has been shining for the last hour, has just gone behind a cloud.

On 29 September 1956, when this picture was taken, all seems to have gone according to plan. After sweeping through Brent station and then around a 90-degree bend, the 'Cornish Riviera Express' is accelerating along a short section of straight track towards the South Devon summit at Wrangaton, behind 4-6-0s Nos 7034 *Ince Castle* and 6025 *King Henry III*.

In the background dark shower clouds are coming off the moor and moving towards Brent Hill, but the train is still well lit. The plume of exhaust steam from the 'Castle' is enough to indicate movement without blotting out the landscape, and also serves to obscure the telegraph pole, which would otherwise be emerging from the chimney of the 'King'.

The 'Castle' is carrying an empty train reporting number frame, having worked the 7.30 am Paddington to Paignton via Bristol train. She was then available at Newton Abbot to pilot the 'Cornish Riviera Express' through to Plymouth, if required, as on this occasion.

23 August 1986

'King'-sized

While browsing through the catalogue of a well-known Austrian manufacturer of model railway equipment, I was struck by the unusual way in which the power output of the various prototypes was expressed. Each class of steam, diesel and electric locomotive was given a power output in kilowatts.

Applying a kilowatt power output to a steam locomotive seems quite strange to one schooled in the traditional British method, which used a formula involving the number and diameter of the cylinders, the length of the piston stroke, the pressure of steam in the boiler, and the diameter of the driving wheels, to produce a somewhat meaningless figure, described as the nominal tractive effort, expressed in thousands of pounds (weight, of course, not sterling).

One of the first railway companies to exploit this formula for publicity purposes was the Great Western Railway, which used it to good effect during the early 1920s on the introduction of the 'Castle' Class, described by the company at that time as 'the most powerful passenger train engine in Great Britain', with a nominal tractive effort of 31,625 lbs.

By 1927 the 'Castles' had been overtaken in terms of tractive effort by the Southern Railway's 'Lord Nelson' Class, and the order came from Sir Felix J. C. Pole, the then General Manager of the GWR, to the locomotive department to build a locomotive that would put the GWR far ahead of the other railway companies. A tractive effort of no less that 40,000 lbs was demanded, sufficient, it was thought, to keep the competition at bay for the next decade.

The 'King' Class 4-6-0s were the result, and the objective was just achieved, but only after increasing the boiler pressure to 250 lbs per square inch, increasing both the bore and stroke of the cylinders and decreasing the GWR's standard wheel size for its express engines from 6 ft $8^1/2$ in to 6 ft 6 in. This last measure was an expensive modification to established practice, and was apparently done solely to achieve the magic figure demanded.

Both wheel size and cylinder bore are subject to some variation during the life of an engine. The wheels will have metal removed on a wheel lathe at each major overhaul in order to restore the correct flange profile, so getting progressively smaller in diameter. The cylinders will be bored out at overhaul to restore them from their slightly oval shape when worn.

Thus it can be seen that any figure quoted on the basis of these supposedly fixed measurements is less than useful, especially in the case of the 'Kings', as it is believed that only the first five were built with the cylinders bored out to the officially quoted $16^1/4$ inches anyway. Later engines started with 16-inch cylinders, which gave the castings a longer life.

However, on the road it is the ability to boil water that counts above mere figures, and GWR boilers were rarely at fault in this respect. Here the last of the class, No 6029 *King Edward VIII* (which was *King Stephen* until May 1936), seems to have no shortage of steam, though not all of it is reaching the cylinders, as the Sunday 'Cornish Riviera Limited' rounds the first part of the S-bend between Stoneycombe and Dainton tunnel on 17 February 1957.

As it storms around the curve, the low winter sun reflects from the smokebox, and the valley reverberates to 135 tons of engine and tender pulling 300 tons of train. With surplus steam oozing from every gland and joint, the working steam expanding in the cylinders forces engine and train up the 1 in 36 gradient to the summit.

6 September 1986

'Mogul' evolution

Without a trace of exhaust from her cast iron chimney, and yawing from side to side with the motion of a ship in a slight swell, 2-6-0 No 7333 climbs steadily up the bank out of Totnes towards Brent. At the rear of this heavy goods train 2-6-2T No 4108, one of the Totnes bankers, is taking her share of the load on 25 June 1959.

In those days, throughout each 24 hours two banking engines were normally on duty at Totnes to assist freight trains on the severe climbs which exist on either side of the station. In the Plymouth direction the gradients vary between 1 in 46 and 1 in 71 on the initial part of the climb as far as Tigley, thereafter easing to between 1 in 65 and 1 in 95. In addition to the severe gradients, the lower part of the climb is beset by severe reverse curves.

No 7333 was one of the final batch of GWR 'Moguls' to be built in 1932, at which time she was number 9311. This batch could always be distinguished by their large side-window cabs, and were originally built with the heavier front end, which had been found necessary to reduce flange wear on the front driving wheels, particularly when working in Cornwall. However, by the time this picture was taken the front end weight had been reduced, enabling them to work over lines from which they had been barred previously, and this batch were then renumbered on to the end of the original series.

The story of the GWR 'Moguls' is said to have begun one day in 1910, when one of G. J. Churchward's drawing office assistants, Mr H. Holcroft, who had recently returned from America, was discussing with his chief the merits of the 2-6-0 wheel arrangement, then very popular in America for general-purpose locomotives. As a result he was later asked by Mr Churchward to lay out the arrangement drawings for a 2-6-0 with 5 ft 8 in wheels, outside cylinders, a Standard No 4 boiler, plus as many standard details as possible.

Within 12 months the first 20 'Moguls' were on the road, and such was their success in the role for which they were intended, as 'maids of all work', that by 1932 there were 342 of them.

Mr Holcroft can also be credited with introducing an essential softening of the stark appearance of the original Churchward designs, which owed much to current American practice and were regarded at the time, not without good reason, as extremely ugly. This was partly due to the vertical drop in the footplating which occurred in front of the cylinders, and to the difference in level between cab and tender. Mr Holcroft suggested turning the front end right angle into a 1 ft 2 in radius curve, and then repeating this under the cab to match the height of the tender.

The change was immediately appreciated as enhancing the look of the engines without any sacrifice of additional weight, and this simple modification soon became standard practice for all new construction of the Churchward standard classes. Perhaps the future popularity of the Churchward generation of GWR locomotives, whose efficiency was now allied to good looks, stemmed from this gentle nod in the direction of aesthetics.

4 October 1986

1930s improvements

During the 1920s and 1930s the Great Western Railway made many improvements to its main lines to the South West, largely funded by Government loans, with the aim of encouraging and developing holiday travel by rail, then the only practicable way to travel for most of the people able to take holidays away from home. Bristol Temple Meads station was rebuilt and considerably extended in 1935, but most of the alterations were concentrated on the section between Cogload Junction and Paignton.

A start had been made on the western end in the mid-1920s when Newton Abbot station was completely rebuilt, and this was soon followed by extensive additions to the siding accommodation at Paignton. Although by the outbreak of war in 1939 there were still only two places between Exeter and Newton Abbot at which one train could overtake another, at Dawlish Warren and Exminster, plans were well advanced for driving a new main line, much of it in tunnel, through the hills between Starcross and Bishopsteignton, to avoid the seawall section, but this was stopped by the war. Plans also existed for separating the Southern and Great Western tracks through Exeter, but these were even less well advanced.

East of Exeter, passing places for stopping trains on the main line were provided at Stoke Canon, Cullompton, Tiverton Junction, Sampford Peverell and Wellington, but the major works completed in the early 1930s were from Norton Fitzwarren through Taunton to Cogload Junction. Between these points quadruple tracks were provided throughout, so that the Barnstaple and Minehead branch trains, which had previously joined the main line at Norton Fitzwarren, now had their own track into Taunton station.

Taunton, as well as having four main-line platforms, also acquired bay platforms at either end to accommodate the branch trains to Yeovil, Chard, Minehead and Barnstaple, which could also be used by the main-line stopping trains to Bristol, Exeter and Castle Cary.

Beyond Taunton the quadruple tracks continued through Creech St Michael to Cogload Junction, where the Bristol and Westbury bound lines parted company, and an impressive steel girder flyover was provided to enable the down Bristol line to pass over the lines to Westbury.

Not yet tackled was the bottleneck created for westbound trains at Norton Fitzwarren, and beyond on the climb to Whiteball tunnel, through the Blackdown hills, which was to cause much delay in the post-war years.

Although not particularly severe in itself, this climb had the effect of slowing down on a single track two flows of trains which had until then had an easy run into Taunton on separate tracks from Bristol, and from London via Westbury. We all know from our experience on the roads the effect this has on a heavy traffic flow, if no 'crawler lane' is provided for the slowest vehicle. On summer Saturdays in the 1950s the railway suffered similarly, and it needed only one train to stop at Wellington to request the assistance of a banking engine to bring all those behind to a halt.

No assistance, however, is required by 'Britannia' Class 4-6-2 No 70024 *Vulcan* which has climbed through Whiteball tunnel on 1 July 1961 with the 13 coaches of the 8.05 am Cardiff to Kingswear, and can now run swiftly down the Culm valley towards Exeter.

18 October 1986

Meals on wheels

It is 7.23 pm on the evening of Friday 31 July 1959, the eve of one of the busiest Saturdays of the year, as ex-GWR 4-6-0 No 6845 *Paviland Grange* crosses Forder viaduct with an unusual train composed almost entirely of ex-GWR restaurant cars, which is an essential prelude to the summer Saturday flow of express trains out of Cornwall.

This train left Paddington's platform 4 at 12.05 pm each Friday during the peak season with the extra restaurant cars, already fully provisioned and staffed, that would be required for the following day's up trains. Over an hour will be spent at Exeter while the cars' gas cylinders are fully charged and water tanks topped up, before proceeding to Newton Abbot, where some cars will be detached. During the night these will be marshalled into the trains on which they will be required on Saturday, while their crews rest in the hostel accommodation provided by the railway on the top floor of Newton Abbot station. Meanwhile, the remaining restaurant cars will be hauled over the South Devon banks to Plymouth and across the Royal Albert Bridge at Saltash into Cornwall.

Forder viaduct is the second in a succession of viaducts which carry the main line across the streams and rivers joining the Tamar estuary, and was built by the GWR when this part of the original Cornwall Railway main line was doubled in 1908. The original single-track main line, opened by the Cornwall Railway in 1859, crossed the land seen in the centre of this picture - and was, in 1959, still in use as a siding - before crossing Forder creek on a timber viaduct and following the river Lynher prior to climbing up to St Germans. When this section between Wearde and St Germans was doubled by the GWR a new line was built further inland where it was easier to find firm footings for the piers of the three massive brick viaducts which were to replace the five timber viaducts on the old line.

In the background can be seen Bull Point and the northern end of the Devonport Dockyard, while in the Hamoaze a motley collection of surplus naval craft, including two aircraft carriers, await disposal. It is many years since the last paddle-steamer beat its way down the river Lynher carrying produce from the gardens of St Germans to Devonport market.

Before arriving at its Truro destination, our train of restaurant cars will pause again at Par, while further cars are detached to go forward to Newquay, arriving there at 9.10 pm, where the crews will retire for the night in surplus ex-GWR 3rd class sleeping cars, kept there for this purpose. The crew of the engine taking this train out to Newquay are not so lucky, as they are required to stay on duty all night marshalling the stock for tomorrow's departures, which include three trains to Paddington.

As they watch the scenery go by while consuming their three-course lunch, tomorrow's passengers will be unaware of the organisation and expense which has gone into providing this much-appreciated service.

25 October 1986

Six-coupled evolution

When railways were in their infancy, in the early years of the 19th century, some of the pioneer locomotive designers were doubtful whether the degree of adhesion between a smooth iron wheel and an equally smooth iron rail would be sufficient to allow a useful load to be hauled. Consequently a few of the earliest colliery locomotives, although carried on smooth wheels, were designed to wind themselves along with a toothed wheel engaged in toothed track. Early experience with the steam locomotive soon showed that complications of this nature were unnecessary, and provided that the route of the railway was reasonably graded, simple adhesion was enough to enable large loads to be hauled and at higher speeds than could ever be attained with a toothed transmission. Subsequently, a more sophisticated form of toothed transmission was developed in the 1870s, for use on mountain railways, where safety is paramount and low speed acceptable.

The celebrated Rainhill Trials, initiated by the Liverpool & Manchester Railway in 1829, were to see the birth of the main-line steam locomotive, as opposed to one suitable only for slow-speed colliery work. This was *Rocket*, entered by George and Robert Stephenson and a now forgotten associate Henry Booth, which for the first time brought together three basic features of locomotive design which can still be found in the monster steam locomotives surviving today.

These features were, first, outside cylinders driving directly on to the driving wheel through a connecting rod; the cylinders of *Rocket* were sharply inclined, but in the Stephensons' very similar *Northumbrian* of 1830 they were brought down to the horizontal position. The second feature was the multi-tubed boiler, and the third the separate water-jacketed fire-box. Still to come was the separate smokebox ahead of the boiler barrel, but already by 1834 the steam locomotive as we know it today was recognisable.

Even before *Rocket*, another of the Rainhill contestants, Timothy Hackworth, had realised that adhesion would be enhanced if all the weight of the locomotive was carried on six coupled wheels, thus producing in his *Royal George* of 1827 a primitive version of what was to become almost the standard type of the latter part of the 19th century - the 0-6-0 tender and 0-6-0 tank engine.

It was the Americans who first found it necessary to add a leading four-wheeled bogie, when the Norris Brothers of Philadelphia adapted the design of the early steam engines imported from England, in order to achieve successful running on the rather roughly-laid American track. First came the 4-4-0, built in immense quantities from the 1850s, and later the 4-6-0.

The basic design features of the American 4-6-0 were brought back to this country by the GWR's famous locomotive engineer G. J. Churchward at the turn of the century and, after a few experiments with various design features, became his 'Saint' Class express passenger 4-6-0s.

In 1924 one of these engines, *Saint Martin*, was rebuilt by his successor, C. B. Collett, with smaller 6 foot driving wheels, to become the first 'Hall' Class engine - ultimately to number 330 examples.

Surefooted as ever, No 4936 *Kinlet Hall* is climbing Dainton bank assisted at the rear of a long goods train by 2-6-2T No 4179, hidden around the curve by the budding branches of the densely wooded slopes of Stoneycombe quarry, on 23 April 1955.

15 November 1986

A busy day at Exeter

The morning of Saturday 23 July 1960 dawned dull and cold, with a thin drizzle in the air that looked like remaining there for the rest of the day. Not the sort of day for touring the overcrowded Devon roads by motor cycle in search of scenic photographs.

A day at Exeter therefore seemed more attractive, and after observing the arrival of the overnight 10.00 pm Friday train from Nottingham rolling into Torquay over 2^1/$_2$ hours late, I travelled up to Exeter on the 7.45 am Paignton to Newcastle behind 4-6-0 No 6829 *Burmington Grange*.

Observing from the corridor of the up Newcastle, it was soon evident why the Nottingham had been so late. The overnight traffic on this peak Saturday had been so intense that a queue had developed, both on the branch and on the run into Newton Abbot. Between Torre and Powderham no fewer than 18 trains were either stopped or slowly easing forward to the next signal.

Most were holiday trains from points as diverse as Manchester (four trains), Hull, Newcastle, Keighley, Rotherham, Bradford, Sheffield (two trains), Derby and Birmingham, but also trapped in the queue were two Exeter to Kingswear locals, down parcels and fish trains, and the midnight Paddington to Penzance sleeper hauled by one of the new 'Warship' Class diesel-hydraulic locomotives; all the other trains were steam-hauled.

When I arrived at Exeter the last of the overnight trains were just coming in. The 6.58 pm Glasgow to Plymouth was behind 4-6-0 No 6978 *Haroldstone Hall*, which, despite being removed to shed for attention, returned to take the train on only 48 minutes late. Then came the last overnight Liverpool and Manchester, which were only 15 and 19 minutes late respectively, behind 'Castle' Class 4-6-0 No 5075 *Wellington*

and 'Warship' Class No D819 *Goliath*.

With four steam-hauled relief trains in front of it, the 7.00 am Paddington to Kingswear was badly delayed and arrived nearly an hour late behind No D815 *Druid*, and this affected following trains.

Much to the consternation of homeward-bound Exeter office workers, for whom the 6.35 am Walsall provided a stopping service from Dawlish to Kingswear, this train arrived 97 minutes late behind 4-6-0 No 6021 *King Richard II*, unusual motive power for this train. By coincidence, within minutes of arriving, *King Richard II* was overtaken by No 6016 *King Edward V*, which thundered past on the centre road with the 13 coaches of the 9.30 am Paddington to Newquay.

Meanwhile, the procession of 'Castles', 'Halls' and 'Granges' on the down trains continued, until relieved at 4.15 pm by the appearance of BR Standard Class '9F' 2-10-0 No 92249 on the 13-coach 11.40 am Paddington to Penzance, which was also immediately overtaken by another engine of the same class, No 92218 on the 7.55 am Rotherham to Paignton relief.

It was still raining at 5.20 pm when the imposing mass of ex-GWR 2-8-0 No 4705 arrived on the 1.20 pm Paddington to Kingswear. As the driver oils around the valve spindle and slide bars, the fireman is pulling coal forward from the back of the tender, and further down the train the dining car is being watered. Just running in on the left is 'Battle of Britain' Class 4-6-2 No 34058 *Sir Frederick Pile* on the 2.55 pm Ilfracombe to Waterloo.

Although we have only looked at the down trains, of which there were 88 by 6.00 pm, altogether over 170 train movements had taken place at Exeter since 9.00 am - it had been a busy day.

13 December 1986

A 'Castle' passes

A watery sun glints through bare branches as ex-GWR 4-6-0 No 5036 *Lyonshall Castle* storms up Dainton bank towards Stoneycombe quarry with the 9.30 am from Paddington to Newquay and Falmouth in February 1956.

From this viewpoint it is possible to hear the approaching train accelerating away from the speed restriction across Aller Junction, and to follow its progress aurally for the next half-mile as its speed at first increases a little, then holds steady as the train comes into view. It is still half a mile away across the valley, and the engine has to work increasingly hard to maintain speed as it sweeps around the long right-hand bend, across the road to Kingskerswell, and on to the embankment approaching our position, which is just below the Stoneycombe quarry siding buffer stop.

The even exhaust beat from the four cylinders of the 'Castle' becomes more insistent as the driver winds the reversing gear nearer to full forward, in a losing battle to defeat the effect of the adverse gradient.

For a few moments there is time to take in the gleaming copper and brasswork of the 'Castle', whose well-oiled green paintwork contrasts with the red of the buffer beam, and the neat rake of coaches, still in the early British Railways livery of carmine and cream. Then, in a crescendo of sound, mostly from the exhausted steam, but some from the lifted safety valves and more escaping from internal joints which are anything but steam-tight, we are left with the aroma of hot oil and the gentle patter of descending cinders, as the passing coach bogies tap out their rhythm on the rail joints.

Once the last vehicle has passed, the staccato beat from the engine exhaust again dominates the valley, now echoing back and forth around the quarry buildings, each beat becoming ever sharper and more distinct, until the 'Castle' disappears around the sharp bend leading to the final 1 in 36 up to the tunnel, and the sound is absorbed by the tree-shrouded hillside.

Lyonshall Castle was one of ten 'Castle' Class engines built at Swindon for the summer traffic of 1935. This practice of building ten new 'Castles' each spring had become something of a habit for the GWR. With a few exceptions - during the Depression years, and in 1928 and 1930, when the even larger 'Kings' were built instead - the company had added at least ten new 'Castles' to stock each year from 1925 to 1939.

After the war, although the locomotive department had plans to produce a new 'Pacific' class of locomotives, this was not approved by the Directors and Swindon resumed production of their annual quota of ten 'Castles' in 1946. This continued until 1950, with the exception of 1947, probably due to the post-war shortages, which were then at their most extreme.

Together with rebuilds from the earlier 'Star' Class, the total number of 'Castles' eventually reached 171, 14 or 15 of which were based at Newton Abbot during the early post-war years.

3 January 1987

Last rites in the snow

The last passenger trains were due to run on the Plymouth to Launceston branch on 29 December 1962, and travelling over the line that morning on the 10.40 am from Plymouth it was already clear that there was likely to be trouble later in the day. Snow had fallen overnight and had covered the exposed parts of the platforms at Plymouth, as the empty stock for our train was brought up from Millbay by 2-6-2T No 5564, both engine and coaches wreathed in steam. Progress on the outward journey was normal, despite the deepening snow at Yelverton, and Tavistock was passed without incident.

Between Tavistock and Lydford the GWR Launceston branch and the Southern Railway main line from Plymouth to Exeter share the same valley, and just beyond Mary Tavy & Blackdown our train was overtaken by a 'West Country' 'Pacific' hauling the Plymouth to Brighton express, which rapidly disappeared into the frozen landscape in a cloud of steam and snow.

At Lydford, high on the northern edge of Dartmoor, the two lines part company and the Launceston branch descends down a relatively sheltered valley to its destination.

Returning through Lydford barely an hour and a half later, on the 12.40 pm from Launceston, it was apparent that conditions were worsening. The wind had picked up, bringing continuous flurries of snow off the moor which were starting to drift across the track in places. Long icicles hung from the station roof, where the morning's thaw had been arrested.

Leaving the train at Marsh Mills, on the outskirts of Plymouth, I took this picture of the 2.10 pm short working from Plymouth to Tavistock behind 0-6-0T No 6430, carrying a wreath on its smokebox door. By this time snow was falling again, and with the by now gale force winds it became a struggle to keep the line open. Only one more train, the 3.05 pm out of Plymouth forming the 5.40 pm from Launceston, was to complete its journey on the branch that day, and this was 3 hours late getting back into Plymouth.

Following this was the 7.10 pm from Tavistock, which had to be held at Bickleigh to cross the very late running 6.20 pm from Plymouth to Launceston behind 2-6-2T No 5568, which did not arrive there until 11.35 pm.

However, once the Launceston train had cleared, and it was possible to send the 7.10 pm from Tavistock on its way, it was found that during its long wait both the engine and train brakes had frozen solid. Soon the engine ran short of water and the fire had to be dropped. The passengers - there were only three - and train crew then retired to the signal box for the rest of the night, where refreshments were served by the Station Master's wife. The other train struggled on to Tavistock, but beyond there the staff token apparatus had broken down and the Southern train which could have brought a pilotman down from Lydford had become stuck in snow near Meldon. The 67 passengers on the 6.20 pm from Plymouth spent the night at Tavistock, either in the station or in emergency accommodation arranged by the WRVS.

Everyone on the line had done their utmost to keep the trains running to the end of the timetable service, but in the end were defeated by the elements. The last trains from either end never even had a chance to start their journeys.

17 January 1987

Heading West

On the last leg of its journey down from Paddington on 13 October 1956, 4-6-0 No 7029 *Clun Castle* accelerates the 'Torbay Express' away from Aller Junction.

The route normally used by non-stop trains to the West Country was described in the pre-war Great Western Railway timetables as being 'via Castle Cary'. This description, however, only dated from 1932, prior to which the timetables showed these trains as running 'via Westbury'. The distinction arose from the completion in 1932 of the double-track avoiding lines, which enabled non-stop trains to bypass the junctions at Frome and Westbury. The completion of these avoiding lines was the final step in converting what had started out as a collection of branch and cross-country lines into the premier trunk rail route to the South West.

In broad gauge days the GWR route to the South West was via Bristol, and the company was in difficulties competing with the London & South Western Railway's shorter route to Exeter. However, once the broad gauge lines had been converted the company set about providing itself with a route to the West Country on which it could compete with the LSWR on more equal terms.

Back in the early days of the GWR, Brunel had had to decide whether to take his line from Bristol to London to the north or to the south of the Marlborough Downs. For his main line he chose the more gentle gradients possible on the northerly route, but when laying out the route for a branch line from Reading to Hungerford to the south, he was already envisaging that this might one day become part of a main line to the West Country, as it is today.

Sadly, he could not have foreseen the speeds which would one day be attained, and today's High Speed Trains snaking up the Kennet valley, crossing and re-crossing both the river and the Kennet & Avon canal, soon show up the line's humble origin. Beyond Hungerford, reached in 1847, the line was extended on over the summit at Savernake and down through the Vale of Pewsey to Devizes, reached in 1862. In the vicinity of Woodborough traces of the old formation of the original single line of the Berks & Hants Extension Railway of 1862 can still be seen on the up side.

Today Devizes is without rails, an eventual victim of the first of the GWR cut-off lines which were soon to convert these rural byways into a main line to the West. The new line connected Patney & Chirton, about 4 miles short of Devizes, with Westbury, and, when it opened in 1900, considerably reduced the journey time from Paddington to Weymouth. It can be identified by its gentle gradient and long sweeping curves, and was well known as a race-track in the down direction in steam days.

Beyond Westbury the West of England main line uses the route planned by the Wilts, Somerset & Weymouth Railway via Frome to Castle Cary. From here another GWR cut-off line via Somerton was constructed in 1905-6 to join the old Bristol & Exeter Railway branch line from Yeovil to Durston, at Curry Rivell junction. Again the contrast can be felt between the sharper gradients and curves of the old line, and the considerable earthworks of the newer section, allowing easier gradients and curves.

At the other end of the Athelney marshes a final cut-off line, also opened in 1906, connected Athelney with a new junction at Cogload, on the Bristol to Taunton main line. The old line via Lyng Halt and Durston was not closed, however, and continued to be used by the Yeovil branch trains until the branch closed in the Beeching era.

7 February 1987

Royal Albert Bridge (2)

The great Isambard Kingdom Brunel's enduring legacy to the West Country is the Royal Albert Bridge at Saltash, seen here from the fourth coach of the 11.10 pm from Manchester to Penzance, hauled by 4-6-0 No 4972 *Saint Brides Hall* on 18 July 1959.

As was mentioned on page 34, 1959 was the bridge's centenary year, and the men in the foreground are probably waiting for the train to pass before going out onto the bridge to inspect the temporary floodlighting, which was installed to illuminate the bridge each evening during that summer only. This was several years before the introduction of the orange high-visibility jacket, which everyone working on the line must now wear. Incidentally, it seems incredible today but when the bridge was first opened to traffic in 1859 it was possible for members of the public to purchase tickets from the booking office at Saltash station which entitled them to walk along the railway track and across the bridge to the St Budeaux side. Trains would, of course, have been few and far between in the early days, and the degree of danger more apparent than real; no doubt the station staff would have prevented them from crossing if a train was due. Naturally, the Cornwall Railway Company accepted no responsibility for the walkers' safety and this facility was withdrawn when traffic increased.

With the centenary in mind, British Railways gave the bridge a full repaint during 1958 and early 1959, being finished in a dull silver colour. For the summer of 1959 only, the ladders and walkways, which normally partially obscure the lettering above the entrance archway at either end, were removed. These ladders give access, through large iron doors, to the interior of the wrought iron tubes from which the suspension chains are hung, and also to the walkway across the top of the tubes.

The lettering 'I. K. BRUNEL, ENGINEER, 1859' was placed there by the Directors of the Cornwall Railway. The letters themselves were cast by the Plymouth Foundry for £15, undercutting the famous Coalbrookdale Iron Works, which had also tendered, by £10.

Although the main structure is still the original, all the approach spans on either side have been replaced over the years. The first to be replaced were the two nearest to Saltash station, on the far side, when the station platforms were lengthened in 1908. Replacement of the remaining 15 spans was commenced in 1928, following a report to the Great Western Board in July 1927 which said that the original wrought iron girders of 1859 were no longer of full strength and that their renewal was necessary at an early date.

Saltash station was, until the opening of the road bridge in 1961, the terminus for all the bus services in that part of east Cornwall, and most passengers for Plymouth would travel onwards on one of the frequent train services. A slower alternative was the steam-driven chain ferry service, also withdrawn in 1961, since when the riverside scene in the lower part of Saltash has changed considerably.

The ferry at the Saltash Passage had a very long history and it is recorded that the Black Prince gave the ferry lease to his batman for services rendered, and in compensation for his losing an eye at the Battle of Poitiers. However, the lease was normally granted to the Burgesses of Saltash from the Duchy of Cornwall.

14 February 1987

Moorswater viaduct

A little to the west of Liskeard lies Moorswater viaduct, one of the most imposing of the many viaducts which carry the old Cornwall Railway main line across the frequent valleys and inlets which obstruct its path down through the peninsula. With an imminent cloudburst threatening above, but almost silhouetted against the clear skies over Bodmin Moor and Caradon Hill to the north, the train on the viaduct is the 6.27 am up stopper from Falmouth to Plymouth, headed by an unidentified 'Hall' Class locomotive on 2 August 1958.

The line below is the northward extension of the Liskeard and Looe branch, from Coombe Junction to Moorswater, which, when this picture was taken, served both the small two-road engine shed at Moorswater (see page 48) and the Clay Works, which processes clay piped down from the mines on Bodmin Moor.

On the right there is a good view of the back of the signal guarding Coombe Junction. Most older Great Western signals were mounted on square wooden posts, but concrete posts, like this one, were tried from 1917 to 1929, surmounted by the usual GWR style of ball-and-spike finial, with the ball painted red. A ladder is attached to the back of the post to enable the lampman, or more likely the Coombe Junction signalman in this case, to climb up to refill the oil lamp and trim the wick as necessary. The arm of the signal, which is facing towards the viaduct, has a white ring attached to its face, indicating that this signal controls the exit from a siding, on to the branch.

The lamp container has a small lens let into the back, known as the backlight, which can be seen by the signalman at night and confirms to him both that the lamp is alight and that the arm, which he cannot see at night, is still in the horizontal position. Were it to drop more than the regulation 5 degrees from the horizontal, the light would be obscured by the corrugated semi-circular plate, which is attached to the spindle on which the arm moves.

When the signalman 'pulls the signal off', the light will disappear; if it does not reappear when he puts the signal back to danger, then something is wrong, a small example of the fail-safe nature of all railway signalling apparatus.

To the left of the signal can be seen two of the piers of the original Brunel viaduct of 1859, which the existing viaduct replaced in 1881. These delicately tapering piers were pierced at each level of the taper by Gothic openings, which reduced the total weight on the foundations without affecting the strength of the structure.

The single broad gauge track was originally supported, 35 feet above the tops of the piers, by a fan of four yellow pine timbers, supported in a cast iron shoe. The upper ends of these timbers supported the main deck of the viaduct, which was also of timber construction.

While Brunel would probably have preferred to have used brick or masonry for the original viaducts, with no fewer than 34 needed between Plymouth and Truro the Cornwall Railway Company could not afford such extravagance and needed a cheaper alternative.

Thus Brunel turned to timber, which in those times was both relatively cheap and of excellent quality, and developed a unique style of viaduct, the last West Country example of which was not replaced until 1934.

21 February 1987

Taunton

The 3.20 pm from Paddington to Kingswear races non-stop through Taunton station at 5.49 pm, 2 minutes early, on Saturday 30 July 1955 behind 4-6-0 No 7033 *Hartlebury Castle*, one of the last batch of 'Castles' to be built, and then only five years old. The draught from the passing train is redistributing the assorted cigarette and crisp packets bestowed upon the track by the Great British Public. On the right ex-GWR 2-8-0 No 3840 stands at the head of the afternoon parcels train from Bristol to Plymouth.

Today the central island platform at Taunton is bare of buildings and the line is normally used only by non-stop trains, although the platform can be brought back into use for passengers in an emergency. In the 1950s all four main platforms and the bay platforms at each corner of the station were fully operational. With branches radiating to Barnstaple, Minehead, Yeovil and Chard, not to mention the stopping trains on the main line, Taunton was a very busy place.

Until the present station was built in the early 1930s, when the tracks were quadrupled from Cogload Junction in the east to Norton Fitzwarren in the west, Taunton must have been an operational nightmare, only saved from chaos by the freight avoiding lines. These enabled goods and some passenger trains to avoid the station altogether, travelling to the south round behind the locomotive depot, which was then approached on foot from the west end of the main down platform, more or less opposite the point from which this picture was taken.

In today's circumstances, with the branches all closed (although the preserved West Somerset Railway still hopes one day to be able to operate their trains on the Minehead line into Taunton), it is understandable that the central island has been closed.

However, now that the new signalling scheme has reduced the main-line tracks to two again, except through the station, this does lead to delays at Cogload Junction when down trains from Bristol and Westbury are arriving together.

However, a delay from the train in front can occasionally work to one's advantage. I recall a Sunday in the early 1950s when four of us were returning on a warm summer evening from a visit to Swindon Works. As there were no refreshments on the train, we were reduced to buying what we could from station buffets. Taunton was easy - travelling near the back of the train, our coach stopped opposite the buffet which, in those days, was open on the down side.

At Exeter the buffet is well forward, opposite the third coach, and we dispatched a 'runner' to purchase four ice-creams. Having had further to go, he was well down the queue and only just managed to get back on to the train as it was leaving. Walking back through the train towards our coach he came to a locked corridor connection. Disaster - trapped with four melting ices! By now the train was passing City Basin Junction and the ices were held out of the window in a desperate effort to keep them cool, collecting cinders and smuts from the engine as they melted. Then, by some lucky chance, the train was checked at Exminster and stopped long enough at the platform for our ice carrier to transfer from one coach to the next - much to the relief of all concerned.

28 February 1987

Bovey memories

Bovey station on a bright but misty morning in February 1959. Only where the sun has penetrated have the fields turned to green and brown, elsewhere a heavy frost still carpets the meadows.

On the side of the corrugated iron lamp hut an official notice advertises the closure of the passenger service on the Moretonhampstead branch from 2 March 1959, after which date we are told alternative bus services will be provided.

'Large Prairie' tank engine No 5183 makes an abrupt and noisy exit from the station with the two-coach 10.15 am from Moretonhampstead, sending a column of condensing steam high into the branches of the avenue of large trees which flank the by then rarely used down platform. Only once a day, at 8.5 am each morning, are two passenger trains scheduled to cross here, although the 2.15 pm from Newton Abbot is timed to cross the returning daily goods train at 2.30 pm.

Time was, 30 and even 40 years before, that Bovey station in summer would have been thronged with visitors arriving by train from Torquay, Paignton and farther afield, alighting here to board the charabancs that would laboriously grind their way up to the moors. Normally open to the sky, but with canvas hoods to keep the weather out, and the condensation in, the 'charas' had bench seats across the body, which was mounted on one of the many lorry chassis made surplus at the end of the 1914-18 war.

The charabancs would be lined up in the station forecourt, part of which can be seen on the right of our picture, with destinations indicated on boards mounted in front of the windscreen: Haytor Rocks, Becky Falls and Manaton. With solid tyres, rough roads, crash gearboxes and primitive braking systems, these journeys were probably quite long enough and no doubt could be exciting at times.

Until 1929 these services were run by the GWR itself, but as by then it had been discovered that the railway had no statutory authority to run the bus services it had already been operating for nearly 30 years, railway bus services were taken over by new companies in which the railways took a share. The GWR services were taken over by the Western National, although Devon General vehicles were used for the moorland services out of Bovey until 1934, when Potter's Tor Bus took over.

But to return to the more peaceful scene in 1959, unusually for a train that has only come a few miles, it is 15 minutes late. Probably time was lost while detaching van traffic at Moretonhampstead, taken out on the rear of the previous train. Not that this lateness will matter very much to any intending long-distance passengers, because beyond sunny South Devon the rest of the country is paralysed by one of the last of the really dense pea-soup fogs.

Back at Newton Abbot the 5.30 am from Paddington to Plymouth is posted as 77 minutes late off Taunton and the up 'Torbay Express' has been cancelled, probably to ease congestion at the London end.

However, thanks to the Automatic Train Control apparatus developed by the GWR, running trains on the main line in fog is not the hazardous operation it had been on some other lines. As if to prove this, 'Castle' Class engine No 5075 *Wellington* coasts through Newton Abbot with an 'Ocean Liner' special containing some of the GWR's special saloons named after members of the Royal Family, and accelerates away past East box into the mist, bound for London.

7 March 1987

Newton Abbot manoeuvres

This unusual scene, on Sunday 4 December 1955, shows the down 'Cornish Riviera Express', headed by 4-6-0 No 6022 *King Edward III*, travelling 'wrong line' down the up through road of Newton Abbot station. It is emerging from the Moretonhampstead branch, and this has, in the past, led to some people who have seen this photograph suggesting that the train had travelled between Exeter and Newton Abbot over the Teign Valley line via Christow and Heathfield.

This would not have been possible, however, with a 'King' Class locomotive, as its $22^{1}/_{2}$-ton axle loading would have been too great for the track and bridges on this line, which was normally used only by 0-4-2 side tanks, 0-6-0 pannier tanks and 2-6-2 tanks of the '45xx' and '55xx' Classes. 'Manor' Class 4-6-0s and '43xx' Class 2-6-0s were specially permitted, with a maximum speed of 25 mph, and it would have been one of these classes which would have been used if the 'Cornish Riviera Express' had been diverted over this route.

On this day, however, the express had come down the normal coastal route, via Dawlish and Teignmouth, to arrive in the down side of Newton Abbot, but beyond the station the Civil Engineer had Sunday occupation of both down tracks, making further progress forwards impossible. Consequently, after detaching the Kingswear coaches, the 'Cornish Riviera Express' had to back out of the station, across in front of the East signal box, sufficiently far down the Moretonhampstead branch to clear the points leading to the up side (the 'King' Class locomotives were permitted on the branch as far as the second river bridge). Having completed this manoeuvre, the train is now leaving the Moretonhampstead branch and proceeding westwards on the 'wrong line', probably as far as either Stoneycombe or Dainton Sidings, before regaining the correct left-hand track. On the right of the picture the passengers in the Kingswear coaches are watching this unusual operation, before being treated to a similar excursion themselves.

The foreground platform was then Newton Abbot station's No 9 platform, the bay normally used by the Moretonhampstead branch trains, and also by the daily through train from Exeter via the Teign Valley line.

The up-side gantry, under which the train is passing, was then complete with 11 arms; eight home signals, controlling the routes available out of the three eastbound tracks, plus three distant signals, applicable only to the main line.

The whole scene is somewhat reminiscent of the months following the D-Day landings in June 1944, when American ambulance trains could be seen emerging from the Moretonhampstead branch into Newton Abbot station after delivering their load of casualties to the American hospital at Stover.

These trains were of particular interest to the railway observers of the time because they were hauled by London & North Eastern Railway 'B12/3' Class 4-6-0 locomotives. Reasonably powerful, but with an axle loading of less than 16 tons, these engines had been designed in 1911 by the Great Eastern Railway for its express services out of Liverpool Street. They were, therefore, an ideal choice for hauling these heavy American ambulance trains to hospitals such as the one at Stover, which could only be approached over either the Teign Valley or Moretonhampstead branch lines, neither suitable for the heavy express locomotives of the Great Western Railway.

14 March 1987

Launceston rivalries

The ancient market town of Launceston, situated astride the A30 road and close to the border between Devon and Cornwall, is an interesting example of the duplication of railway facilities which persisted in many towns throughout the period of company ownership of the railways.

By the time this picture was taken, on 2 March 1954, passenger traffic had been concentrated on the former Southern Railway station and the Great Western Railway station alongside had been closed to passengers. Until dictated by wartime necessity in 1943, there had been no rail connection between the two stations, although they occupied adjacent sites and their approach tracks crossed each other outside the town.

The reason for this lay deep in the railway history of the South West peninsula, dominated always by the intense 19th-century rivalry between the Great Western and the London & South Western railway companies.

Around the middle of the 19th century Launceston was a town in decline. It had lost its Assizes in 1838, and by 1860 viewed with envy the increasing importance of Tavistock to the south, which became the terminus of the broad gauge South Devon & Tavistock Railway from Plymouth in 1859.

Proposals had already been made for railways to Launceston from both Tavistock and Okehampton, but each had failed and the town's only route for heavy materials remained via the Bude Canal to Druxton Wharf, some 4 miles distant.

In 1861 a new Parliamentary Bill was introduced, with the support of the LSWR, for a railway to Launceston from Copplestone, on the North Devon line. This was successfully opposed by the broad gauge companies, which then proposed their own extension of the existing broad gauge line from Tavistock under the guise of the Launceston & South Devon Railway. This Bill was successful, and with few constructional problems the line was opened in July 1865.

Several further attempts were made to obtain a connection to the LSWR's system, but each failed, and it was not until 1886 that Launceston became the temporary terminus of a standard gauge line from Halwill Junction, operated by the LSWR and later extended to Wadebridge and Padstow.

Until 1892 the two lines were of different gauges, but from that year until 1947 the two stations operated side by side, each with full passenger and goods facilities, each with its own engine shed and turntable, and competing for the available traffic. Following nationalisation in 1948 came the first attempts to rationalise the situation, and from 1952 all the ex-GWR passenger trains from Plymouth were diverted into the ex-SR station via the wartime connection, the first regular use to be made of this facility.

Thus our 1954 picture shows the trains from both lines in the ex-Southern station. On the left ex-GWR 2-6-2T No 4530 waits with the two-coach 2.10 pm train for Plymouth. Just leaving the station on the 12.45 pm from Padstow to Waterloo is ex-SR 'N' Class 2-6-0 No 31842.

Little has changed since company days. The 2-6-0 has added a '3' to its old Southern Railway number and now sports the latest British Railways black livery, lined out in red, cream and grey, but it is passing a London & South Western Railway bracket signal, stoutly constructed from old rail and topped with two typical lattice posts.

21 March 1987

Atmospheric Starcross

The high tide in the river Exe laps gently against the wall as ex-GWR 4-6-0 No 6025 *King Henry III* hurries through with the 8.00 am Kingswear to Paddington train on 29 July 1961.

The residents of the riverfront houses in Starcross give the train only a passing glance, but expectation in the village must have been at fever pitch on Whit Saturday, 30 May 1846, when the first South Devon Railway train from Exeter to Teignmouth rumbled into the station headed by a 2-2-2 locomotive hastily hired from the Great Western Railway. After all, trains had been promised for the previous July, but winter storms had held up work on the exposed seawall section and the mud of Cockwood Harbour had proved to be too deep for the proposed embankment.

Many residents must have been surprised to see a locomotive at the head of the first train, for had not the South Devon Railway opted for the Atmospheric System of propulsion, as recommended by Isambard Kingdom Brunel? Indeed, the company had done so, but the Atmospheric System was not yet ready, and the Directors of the railway were keen to see some revenue coming into their coffers. In this they were not disappointed, as Exeter people flocked to use the new railway to travel down to the coast.

But what of the Atmospheric System, whose historic relic, the remains of the Pumping Engine House at Starcross, can be seen on the left of our picture? Truth to tell, work on it was way behind Mr Brunel's optimistic schedule, which had promised a start to services using the Atmospheric System in July 1845.

By the spring of 1846, work on installing the pipe between the rails had only proceeded as far as Dawlish, and it was to be almost another 12 months before the six engine houses as far as Teignmouth were complete.

Readers will probably be aware of the principle on which the system worked, with the piston carriage acting as locomotive to the train. The air in the pipe between the rails was exhausted from in front of the train by the stationary engines in the pumping houses every 3 miles, and the atmospheric pressure behind the piston forced the train along. For the piston below the piston carriage to enter the pipe, a slot had to be left in the top of the pipe, and it was keeping this slot sealed that proved to be the downfall of the system.

However, it must be said that during its early months the Atmospheric System was very successful and far more trains gained time than lost it. Had it not been for the fact that Brunel seriously underestimated the power needed to exhaust the pipe, so that the stationary engines had always to be run beyond their designed speed, at great expense in coal, more effort might have been put into solving the problem of the seal, a possible solution for which was already in sight.

But the shareholders had had enough of promises, and at a meeting in January 1849 they decided to abandon the 'Atmospheric Caper', as it had come to be known. No longer would smoke pour from the Italianate chimney tower above the Starcross Engine House. Nor could small boys any longer watch in awe the enormous 25-foot-high engine oozing steam as 30 times a minute the piston rose and fell 6 feet, driving the huge 24-foot flywheel, and exhausting the contents of 3 miles of 15-inch pipe into the roof of the building.

Despite the rumble of the trains, Starcross must have seemed a sadly quiet village in 1849.

28 March 1987

Last day at Bovey

This view of Bovey station is taken looking towards Newton Abbot, as the 7.50 am from Newton Abbot leaves for Moretonhampstead on 28 February 1959, the last day of regular passenger services. In the distance the 7.50 am from Moretonhampstead can be seen pulling away towards Newton Abbot behind 2-6-2T No 5196. The usual single auto-coach has been replaced by three non-corridor compartment coaches to cater for the large number of passengers expected later in the day.

On arrival at Moretonhampstead 0-4-2 tank No 1466 will have 9 minutes in which to run around the train and take water, before returning as the 8.40 am to Newton Abbot. This was a variation on the practice of previous years, when this train ran through to Paignton and then did a return trip to Moretonhampstead and back to Newton Abbot, arriving at 12.09 pm.

With impending closure, the timetable planners had deleted this working entirely, and after No 5196 had made the only trip of the day advertised to convey both 1st and 2nd class passengers, which was the 9.20 am down from Newton Abbot and 10.15 am back, there was now a gap in the service until 12.50 pm.

Consequently, on this last day this train was full, with many standing passengers, as little No 1466 struggled up the rising gradients beyond Bovey, starting a number of lineside fires on the way. This was to be her final trip on the branch, as subsequent trains were increased in length and entrusted to another of the 'Large Prairie' tanks, No 4117, which had been specially polished up for the occasion. She handled the 2.15 pm, 4.25 pm, 6.05 pm and the final 8.15 pm departure from Newton Abbot's No 9 bay platform, amid the popping of many flashbulbs. Normally the 8.15 came back as empty

stock, but on this occasion passengers were carried, so that people from Newton Abbot could travel on the last train.

The residents of Moretonhampstead and Lustleigh, who had supported the branch well in its latter years, turned out in large numbers, whole families taking a last ride on their railway, to say goodbye to a line which, if it had been properly promoted, would never have closed. As it was, the economics barely supported closure, and a recommendation was made that diesel railcars should be tried out, when these became available. This was never done.

The first 4 miles of the line, to just beyond Heathfield, are still open for freight traffic, and with only a further 8 miles of single track onwards to Moretonhampstead, a through service of diesel railcars between Kingswear and Moretonhampstead, properly supported by a campaign to promote this as an alternative access to Dartmoor, would surely have covered the additional maintenance costs. Sadly, the days of the basic railway were still in the future, and closure proposals always envisaged continuing the branches on their existing cost basis.

But to end on a happier note, 0-4-2T No 1466 went on to work on the Brixham branch before being transferred to Exeter for service on the Exe Valley line, finally ending her service with British Railways at Taunton, working the shuttle service between Tiverton Junction and Tiverton.

From here she was purchased by the Great Western Society, spending four years at Totnes before travelling under her own steam to the Society's new base at Didcot, where she can still be seen, unless on temporary loan to another preservation site.

18 April 1987

Morning at St Ives

In these days, when the dwindling number of locomotives needed to keep Britain's trains running tend to be concentrated in large numbers at a relatively few locations, it seems a world away from the days when there was a locomotive depot to be found at the end of almost every branch line.

Typical of these little single-engine depots was this one at St Ives in Cornwall. Built originally to house a broad gauge tank engine, it has the familiar 'wide open mouth' appearance which betrays a building designed for the Brunel gauge. No doubt it would once have had wooden doors, but the doors to St Ives shed had long since gone when this picture was taken in the early morning of Saturday 9 September 1961, the day this shed was due to close - not because the line was closing, but because diesels were taking over the service the following week.

The St Ives branch was conceived by the West Cornwall Railway, and was the last branch to be built to Brunel's 7 ft 0$\frac{1}{4}$ in gauge, opening on 1 June 1877. The original occupant of this shed would probably have been one of the broad gauge 4-4-0 saddle tanks, but following the gauge conversion in 1892 the St Ives branch became the preserve of two unique Great Western engines, the 0-4-4 tanks Nos 34 and 35.

Originally built as 0-4-2 saddle tanks, they were evidently not a success and were soon rebuilt as 0-4-4s with very short side tanks. It seems likely that they were still not very useful engines, as No 35 was condemned in 1906 after a very short life, and No 34 was sold two years later to a dealer. He re-sold the engine to the Military Railway at Longmoor in Hampshire, and there it lasted until 1921, when it was sent to Swindon Works for repair, but was found to be worn out and scrapped. One reason for the short life of Nos 34 and 35 may

have been that by 1905 Wolverhampton Works was already turning out the first of ten Churchward-designed 2-6-2 tanks, specifically for use on the tortuous branch lines of the South West. Certainly by the early 1920s both Helston and St Ives were each allocated one of these very useful engines - No 4403 at Helston and No 4408 at St Ives.

In later years the '44s' in West Cornwall were sent north, not far from their birthplace, to work the steeply graded line from Wellington (Salop) to Much Wenlock and Craven Arms, where their tiny 4 ft 1$\frac{1}{2}$ inch driving wheels must have been invaluable.

They were replaced in West Cornwall by their larger-wheeled brethren, the '45xx' Class, which continued to give sterling service on these lines until the end of steam. It is one of this class, No 4564, which is seen here just after emerging from the still gas-lit shed into the early morning sunshine.

Overnight the shedman has raked out the ashpan and cleared any accumulated ash and clinker from the firegrate, before re-lighting the fire and gradually building it up. He will also have cleaned out the smokebox and lanced the tubes, before topping up the bunker with coal.

When the early turn driver and fireman came on duty, the engine would still have been in the shed. After first oiling round, the driver would have moved the engine out and placed it under the water column, so that the tanks could be filled. In another half-hour the fire will have brought the steam up to full working pressure and No 4564 will be ready for the day's work ahead.

25 April 1987

Meeting at Totnes

On the approach to Totnes from the Plymouth direction, as seen from the bypass road bridge, two trains cross at 5.25 pm on 4 October 1958. On the left, running downhill into Totnes, is ex-Southern Railway unrebuilt Bulleid 4-6-2 No 34035 *Shaftesbury* - temporarily minus its nameplate on this side - at the head of the 4.32 pm all stations except Exminster stopping train from Plymouth to Exeter.

This train has already called Plympton, Cornwood, Ivybridge, Bittaford Platform, Wrangaton and Brent, connecting at the latter place with the 4.05 pm from Kingsbridge, which was itself a connection with the 3.30 pm Western National omnibus (Heavy luggage not conveyed) from Salcombe.

A van loaded with local produce would often be transferred at Brent from the front of the Kingsbridge branch train to the back of the up stopper, and would later be shunted again at Exeter, and put into one of the three Perishables trains which carried West Country produce daily to the markets of London and the North.

The working of a Southern Region engine over Western Region tracks between Plymouth and Exeter was a regular feature of the post-Second World War years, and together with a corresponding working of a Western Region engine, usually a '63xx' Class 2-6-0, over the Southern Region route via Okehampton, enabled the engine crews of both Regions to maintain their knowledge of each other's route. This was essential during the war years, when this practice was initiated, in case either route was blocked by enemy action, in the days when the railway was the main supply route for all essential materials, both military and civilian.

During the war years these exchange workings, as they were usually known, extended to two passenger and one goods train each weekday, the Southern Railway normally providing 'N' Class 2-6-0s, as the first of the lightweight Bulleid 'Pacifics' did not appear until 1945.

Leaving Totnes station and commencing the climb up past Tigley to Rattery, and on to Brent, is ex-GWR 4-6-0 No 4948 *Northwick Hall* on the 9.05 am Liverpool (Lime St) to Plymouth express. Now approaching the end of its long and, by today's standards, rather leisurely journey, the train is down probably to eight coaches, well within the capacity of a 'Hall' over the South Devon banks. But earlier in the day, between Shrewsbury and Newton Abbot, the train will have been a full 14-coach load behind a 'Castle' Class 4-6-0, as during this part of the journey it also conveyed through coaches from Manchester (London Road), departing 9.10 am, for Torquay, Paignton and Kingswear.

Any passengers for the Kingsbridge branch are in for a long wait, as their connection does not leave Brent until 6.45 pm, 65 minutes after their arrival, which looks like being on time.

A link with the earliest days of the railway is the tall chimney of Daws Creameries whose building adjoining the station was built to house the pumping engines for the South Devon Railway's Atmospheric System of propulsion (see also page 82), which had been abandoned before it reached Totnes. Because of this, the GWR, whose engines were used to haul the early South Devon Railway trains, established a locomotive shed at Totnes in 1847, where the engines that were used to bank the goods trains were kept. The site of this shed, which was closed in 1904, lay behind the advertising hoarding on the right, roughly adjacent to the second coach of the train from Liverpool, and was still in use as a siding in 1958.

2 May 1987

Overnight to Paignton

The unusual sight of a down overnight express approaching Torre station through the long, neatly trimmed cutting, double-headed by two smokebox-leading tank engines was enough to produce instant camera action on 9 August 1958.

During the late 1950s most of the Paignton-bound overnight expresses that arrived at Newton Abbot from about 7.00 am onwards had their engines replaced by fresh engines off shed, already prepared for their return journeys later in the morning; these usually came down to Paignton tender-first. However, this train, the 10.30 pm Friday from Manchester Victoria, has had its train engine replaced by two Newton Abbot tank engines, 'Small Prairie' No 5533 and 'Large Prairie' No 4174. The first engine is only going as far as Torquay, where it will be detached and remain as one of the two Torquay bankers. No 5533 was in action almost immediately, and passed through Torre station on the rear of the 8.52 am Paignton to Leeds train (see page 30) within 21 minutes of this picture being taken.

Some people are surprised at the density of rail traffic on the branch in the 1950s, and although the line was very intensively used throughout each summer Saturday, the period from 7.30 am to 9.30 am was often the most difficult for arriving trains. The already delayed overnight down trains contained stock and engines needed for the morning departures from the branch, but they were still further delayed on their way down from Newton Abbot by congestion at Paignton and also, as the up traffic developed, by bankers occupying the line returning from Torre to Torquay. It was not unknown for trains to take over an hour to reach Torre from Newton Abbot in these circumstances, after stopping at almost every signal on the way.

This particular morning I was catching the 9.05 am Paignton to Manchester (London Rd) train, due to leave Torre at 9.20 am, and was quite surprised to find 'Castle' Class 4-6-0 No 5076 *Gladiator* noisily barking its way up from Torquay with 11 coaches in tow, without the aid of a banker. This was quite a load for a 'Castle' up the 1 in 55 from Torquay, not to mention the re-start from Torre.

Some idea of the congestion on the down road can be gained from the trains we passed between Torre and Aller Junction that morning. Arriving at Torre as we left was No 7909 *Heveningham Hall* (tender first) on the 9.05 pm Newcastle, running 57 minutes late. At Scott's Bridge we passed No 4978 *Westwood Hall* on the 11.15 pm Manchester Victoria, running 87 late. Standing in Kingskerswell station was No 7001 *Sir James Milne* with the 8.00 am local from Exeter, already 38 late, and waiting at Aller was No 5985 *Mostyn Hall* on the 12.08 am Manchester (London Rd) to Paignton, only 27 late, but with furthest to go.

However, for me this picture recalls a far less normal day, 3 April 1944, during the run-up to D-Day, when I stood on this bridge and watched as two heavy freight trains crossed beneath; creeping at a snail's pace down the hill, from the Newton Abbot direction, came a triple-headed 40-wagon loaded coal train behind 2-6-2T No 5150, 4-6-0 No 6834 *Dummer Grange* and 2-8-2T No 7222, and while this monster load, with its brake blocks protesting loudly, continued slowly on its way, up from Torre came 2-8-0 No 3837 piloting 4-6-0 No 6814 *Enborne Grange* on 41 vans. A truly memorable sight.

6 June 1987

Southern trio

Even in the unusual circumstances of wartime, it was exceptional to find three engines at the head of either a passenger or a goods train, and even less likely in peacetime.

However, there was one section of line in Devon where the sight of three engines on a passenger train, if not commonplace, could be seen fairly regularly during the mid to late 1950s. This was between Exeter Central and Yeoford, the trains involved being the 11.39 am Exeter Central to Ilfracombe and the 11.35 am Plymouth Friary to Waterloo, in both cases on peak summer Saturdays only.

The reason for this over-provision of motive power on what were often only four-coach trains was 'unbalanced' locomotive workings - that is, locomotives that had useful work to do in one direction only, and then had to get back to their depot. Rather than occupy valuable track space by travelling on their own, in this case back to Exmouth Junction depot, the 'spare' engines are worked back on the front of a service train going in the right direction.

The train in this picture, seen standing in platform No 3 at Exeter St David's station on 9 August 1958 is the 11.35 am from Plymouth Friary to Waterloo, which would have left Plymouth with only the third engine, 'Battle of Britain' Class 4-6-2 No 34060 *25 Squadron* at its head. The second engine, 'U' Class 2-6-0 No 31610 and the leading engine, '700' Class 0-6-0 No 30317 both joined the train at Yeoford.

The 2-6-0 had previously worked the 8.25 am Ilfracombe to Manchester as far as Barnstaple Junction, probably assisting the Western 'Mogul' that would take this train on to Taunton. It then hauled the 10.37 am Barnstaple Junction to Yeoford passenger, terminating there, where it joined the 0-6-0, which had worked the morning goods out to Lapford.

All three will leave the train on arrival at Exeter Central and travel together up the Southern main line the mile or so back to Exmouth Junction shed. Meanwhile, the fresh engine which is to take the train on to London will back on with the restaurant car, before leaving at 2.30 pm for Sidmouth Junction, where further through coaches from Sidmouth will be attached to make up the full load for Waterloo.

The three locomotives make an interesting contrast, spanning 48 years of locomotive design, from the '700' Class 0-6-0 in front, originally designed for the London & South Western Railway by Dugald Drummond and built by Dubs & Company of Glasgow in 1897, to the 'Battle of Britain' Class lightweight 'Pacific' at the rear, a design first introduced for the Southern Railway in 1945 by Mr O. V. S. Bulleid.

Appropriately, between them is sandwiched the 'U' Class 2-6-0, built for the Southern Railway in 1928 to a design by Mr R. E. L. Maunsell. Originally numbered A610, this engine was ordered in 1926 as the first of a further batch of 'River' Class 2-6-4 tanks, to be named *River Beaulieu*. However, the derailment of No A800 *River Cray* at Sevenoaks in 1927, due to instability on the poor quality Southern Railway track of the time, led to the whole class being converted to 2-6-0 tender engines, and No A610 was turned out as an unnamed 2-6-0 in the following year.

13 June 1987

Teignmouth 'Hall'

Only the boys suspend operations on the climbing frame to watch as a rather grubby 'Hall' Class locomotive sweeps around the reverse curves past Teignmouth docks and on under the Shaldon bridge; the girls continue to swing as if unaware of the 500 tons or so of engine and train passing just a few yards away. On their playground, where the warm August sunlight is rapidly being extinguished by the lengthening shadows, the children are sheltered from the stiff north-westerly breeze which is turning back the leaves on the trees beyond the cricket ground.

A few yachts swing on the turning tide, and two seagulls still find a perch on the skeletal remains of the wrecked barge, which is almost completely submerged as the waters lap the estuary wall for a while. In the background, lit by the strong evening sunlight, the Teignmouth riverfront is alive with small craft, including a large yacht moored alongside the still busy shipyard.

The docks, still rail rather than road served in those days, and relatively undeveloped, are only just visible above the tail of the train, which is a Fridays-only extra, the second part of 'The Devonian', the 10.15 am from Bradford to Paignton. Made up of 13 coaches of mixed GWR and LMSR parentage, it is hauled by ex-GWR 4-6-0 No 5987 *Brocket Hall* on 1 August 1958.

The GWR 'Hall' Class originated in 1924, although the first new 'Hall' did not emerge from Swindon Works until 1928. The 1924 engine was a rebuild of 4-6-0 No 2925 *Saint Martin*, which had its 6 ft 8^1/$_2$ inch driving wheels replaced with smaller ones of 6 foot diameter, in response to a Running Department request for a stronger mixed traffic locomotive than the existing '4300' Class 2-6-0s, but with a leading bogie.

The eventual need for such a type had been envisaged by Mr G. J. Churchward back in 1901, when he produced his plan of the standard classes needed to take the GWR over the next 20 years until his retirement, but there was no move to produce one until after he had gone.

Indeed, there are those who would argue that a modernised 'Saint' would have done all that a 'Hall' could do, and a 'Saint' with a larger boiler would have been as good as, and cheaper to run, than a four-cylinder 'Castle'.

Nevertheless, the new Chief Mechanical Engineer, Mr. C. B. Collett, did not move in that direction, and chose to modify the 'Saint' design to that of the 'Halls', of which 330 were eventually built up to 1950.

This of itself is an indication of their success as genuine mixed traffic engines, and with the departure of Mr W. A. Stanier from the GWR to become Chief Mechanical Engineer of the LMSR, the type became a model for one of this country's most numerous locomotive classes of all time, the 'Black Fives' of the LMSR, of which 842 were built.

20 June 1987

Exeter West

Standing under the signal gantry at the west end of Exeter St David's station on a rather wet February day in 1958, 4-6-0 No 5024 *Carew Castle* waits patiently as sister engine No 5078 *Beaufort* leaves, dead on time, at 2.57 pm with the down 'Torbay Express' bound for Kingswear, first stop Torquay station.

Beaufort is accelerating confidently, without trace of a slip, out over the complicated crossings which take the ex-Southern Railway tracks across the ex-GWR main line and up the steep climb to Exeter Central station. Dominating the background is Exeter West signal box, erected in 1913 when St David's station lost its overall roof and was rebuilt into its present form. Apparently intended at the time only as a temporary structure, this signal box, held together by innumerable coats of paint, lasted to the end of mechanical signalling in the Exeter area in May 1985.

Still with its original frame consisting of 118 levers when this picture was taken, a new 131-lever frame was installed in 1959, extending its life for another 26 years.

However, even this should not be the end, as the box was carefully dismantled by an enthusiastic team of signalling experts who have plans for its re-erection at Crewe. Here they hope to re-create the atmosphere of a busy summer Saturday by electronic means, and give the public a chance to experience for themselves the hectic but ordered clamour of a busy junction signal box in the 1950s.

Carew Castle is waiting to leave on the 3.05 pm stopping train to Kingswear, giving a good connection for all the intermediate stations to Torquay not served by the 'Torbay Express', and also acting as the school train for some home-going scholars on the branch.

Standing this close to a large steam engine when the fire is hot and the safety valves are about to lift is not the best place to be on most railways, where the use of 'pop' safety valves gives one no warning of what is to come. The sudden 'pop' as the valves lift, and the subsequent violent hiss of high-pressure steam escaping to the atmosphere, developing into a nerve-shattering roar if not immediately attended to by the fireman, is not to be recommended for the well-being of delicate ear-drums.

Great Western Railway engines with their polished brass bonnets, enclosing two direct spring-loaded safety valves, had much better manners and gave due warning of what might be about to follow, by commencing with an apologetic sizzle. But even they could make a tremendous din if the fireman was either careless, or perhaps on occasion caught out by an unexpected delay, with a hot fire and a full boiler. However, a good fireman would endeavour to keep steam pressure in the boiler up to, or just below, the sizzle point, so that the driver always had use of the full capacity of the engine without any wasteful loss of valuable water, on which the engine ultimately depends for further progress.

4 July 1987

Rails through Cornwall

Although the route of the present-day main line through Cornwall was surveyed by Isambard Kingdom Brunel, its almost continuous curves and gradients bear little resemblance to the great man's 'billiard table' route from Bristol to London, which had been completed but a few years earlier.

When surveying the original route of the Great Western Railway, Brunel clearly had doubts as to whether the steam engines of the day would be able to haul an economic load up any but the gentlest of gradients. Indeed, some of the locomotives built rigidly to his own specification were barely capable of moving themselves, still less of hauling a useful load. But then locomotive design seems to have been one of his rare blind spots.

However, by 1845, when the Bill for the proposed Cornwall Railway was presented to Parliament, Brunel evidently had more faith in the rapidly developing steam locomotive, and proposed a double-track line from Plymouth to Truro containing many gradients, but in general nowhere steeper than 1 in 60.

In order to maintain this very reasonable gradient profile through a county of steep wooded valleys, over a route crossed at frequent intervals by rivers and streams making their way to the sea, meant building the railway along the hillside contours and then leaping across the valleys on a succession of magnificent viaducts, the highest of which is St Pinnock, looking down today on Trago Mills from a height of 151 feet.

The contour-hugging curves, with the minimum of long cuttings, and the viaducts giving unobstructed views of the Cornish landscape between them make the journey through Cornwall one of the most rewarding rail rides in the country. But this was just an accidental by-product of Brunel's search for the cheapest way to bring the benefits of the railway age to a county which at that time could only communicate commercially with the rest of the kingdom by sea.

In the event, the proposed double-track line could only be built at first as a single line, and even for this the company had the greatest difficulty raising the required capital.

It is an even stranger quirk of railway history that, but for a last-minute dash from London to St Austell - to Exeter by special one-coach train in $4^1/2$ hours and thence by post chaise to St Austell in $7^1/2$ hours - by William Pease, steward to Cornwall Railway Chairman J. T. Treffry, to deposit the plans on the last possible day for that session of Parliament, the opposition might have won the day. Then the first railway into Cornwall would have been via Okehampton, Launceston and Bodmin, with nearly 3 miles of tunnel and 8 miles of deep cuttings - a much less appealing prospect for the traveller than today's grand entry into the Duchy over the Royal Albert Bridge.

The picture shows Penzance-based 4-6-0 No 5972 *Olton Hall* racing up St Austell bank with an exuberance not often seen in Devon, on the Saturdays-only Carmarthen to Penzance express on 2 August 1958.

11 July 1987

Parcels and Perishables

Headed by 4-6-0 No 7024 *Powis Castle*, the 2.00 pm Perishable train from Penzance to Crewe is crossing the lane leading down to Combe Fishacre from Ipplepen on the final assault of Dainton Bank, where it is due to pass the signal box at 7.19 pm on 7 August 1958.

In those days this was the second of three Parcels and Perishables trains which climbed the bank each weekday evening, the first being the 4.25 pm Parcels train from Plymouth's Millbay station to Paddington via Bristol. Unusually for a Parcels train, and although not shown in the public timetables, it was allowed to carry passengers between Plymouth's North Road station and Newton Abbot, and consequently one passenger coach was always included in the train. As well as its stops for loading parcels at Brent, where a van from Kingsbridge might be attached, and Totnes, the train also stopped at Cornwood to set down passengers, and was due to pass Dainton signal box at 5.51 pm.

In the late 1940s, when many Parcels vans were still branded for specific services, the working timetable showed the actual numbers for some of the vans to be used on this train; on alternate days 'Fruit D' vans Nos 2887 or 2902 would be attached at Newton Abbot from Kingswear, and 'Siphon G' vans Nos 2930 or 2978 from Plymouth were attached at Bristol, after travelling up on the 2.20 pm from North Road to Newton Abbot and then on the 5.15 pm from Newton Abbot to Bristol. On Mondays only, a Tobacco van was carried from Plymouth to Paddington, and every day a Loco Department van, bound for Swindon, was carried between Plymouth and Bristol, identifiable by the large letters 'ENPARTS' on its side.

The subject of our picture, the 2.00 pm from Penzance to Crewe, carried perishable traffic from Cornwall to markets in London, the Midlands and the North of England, with through vans from Penzance for Paddington, Carlisle, Leeds, Manchester, Bristol, Cardiff and Birmingham. The Paddington van was detached at Tavistock Junction to go forward on the following 3.45 pm train from Penzance, which gave a faster service to Paddington, while the Birmingham van came off at Taunton to go forward on the 11.20 pm to Birmingham. At Bristol, the Cardiff and Bristol vans were detached, the former proceeding on the 1.05 am Bristol to Cardiff passenger train, while further vans for Crewe, Carlisle and Manchester were added.

In 1950 this train also carried passengers for a short distance, when it carried school-children between St Austell and Par. Although it is still carrying a passenger coach next to the engine in 1958, there is no mention in that year's service timetables of passengers being carried, but it is possible the practice still continued.

Mention has already been made of the third train, which was due to pass Dainton at 8.40 pm. In 1958 this was the 3.40 pm Penzance to Paddington Perishables, making a fast run to the capital via Castle Cary and due in Paddington at 2.00 am, in good time for traffic to be conveyed to Smithfield and Billingsgate markets, via the Underground Circle line, behind one of the '97xx' pannier tanks fitted with condensing gear for working through the tunnels.

In those days, when the A38 was barely more than a country lane, these three trains were just a fragment of the vast network of interlinking services which daily carried the nation's fruit, fish and general market produce from source to consumer.

18 July 1987

Saturdays from Newquay

High above the valley of the river Fowey, on that spectacular section of the Cornish main line between Largin and St Pinnock viaducts, two of the popular ex-GWR 'Grange' Class 4-6-0s are exerting maximum effort on the coupling of the first coach of train number 638, the 10.00 am from Newquay to Paddington on 2 August 1958.

Loaded to 15 coaches, including a few Churchward 70-footers and a twin diner set, this was usually the heaviest of the many Saturdays-only trains coming out of Cornwall in the 1950s, regularly exceeding the 14 coaches of the 'Cornish Riviera Express'.

This may seem surprising to anyone who knows the exceedingly tortuous and heavily graded nature of the Newquay branch, but it was necessary in order to make the best use of the long single-line section between Tolcarn Junction, just outside Newquay, and St Blazey, broken only by short double-track sections between St Dennis Junction and Tregoss Moor, and between Bugle and Goonbarrow Junction, with additional crossing points at St Columb Road, Roche and Luxulyan.

Nevertheless, despite the then numerous crossing places, the capacity of the Saturday trains to carry people out of Newquay in the peak weeks of the season was often below the number wishing to travel, and overcrowding was commonplace. This train, probably carrying around 800 passengers, was the first of three Saturday trains from Newquay to Paddington. It was preceded by through trains to Manchester and Newcastle, and followed by departures to York, Wolverhampton and Cardiff, together taking about 5,000 people out of Newquay each peak Saturday.

Both ends of the Newquay branch commenced life as mineral tramways built by J. T. Treffry in the middle 1840s. These were taken over by the Cornwall Minerals Railway in 1873, and rapidly upgraded into a line suitable for locomotive working by the following year. This included a formidable gradient up the Luxulyan valley, passing under the viaduct built for the original tramway, which remains to this day an obstacle to down trains proceeding out to Newquay.

Even the diesel locomotives have been known to falter on this bank, and I was once behind one of the Swindon-built diesel-hydraulic 'Warship' Class which stalled on reaching the summit tunnel at Luxulyan. Fortunately it was able to get going again after the second man had walked forward putting ballast on the track. But in steam days it needed three locomotives, two at the front with another at the rear, to lift the 12 coaches of the 9.30 am from Paddington up Luxulyan bank.

Trains from Newquay came down Luxulyan bank, and their most difficult climb was on the main line up to Doublebois, which Nos 6858 *Woolston Grange* and 6849 *Walton Grange* are surmounting in fine style. After $4\frac{1}{2}$ miles the gradient has eased a little at this point, but there is still another mile at 1 in 90 before passing Doublebois station signals the commencement of a mainly downhill run to Plymouth. As this train is not scheduled to stop at Plymouth, it will run through North Road station to Laira Junction, where the train engine will be replaced by a 'King' Class 4-6-0 for the long run up to London, with a pilot engine continuing to give assistance over the South Devon banks to Newton Abbot.

25 July 1987

Bank Holiday Excursions

The words 'Excursion Traffic' have largely been dropped from the local railwayman's vocabulary in recent years. But over most of the railway's history this traffic played a very large part in the activities and income of our local railways during the summer months, and especially around the August Bank Holiday weekend. 1957 was no exception, and following a very busy Saturday, which saw relief trains overnight to Paignton from Congleton, Kidsgrove, Loughborough, Wolverhampton, Leicester, Stoke, Derby and Leeds, followed by day relief trains from Kidderminster, Bristol, Birmingham New Street, Swansea, Leicester and West Hartlepool, all mainly devoted to the carriage of people coming for a week or a fortnight's holiday. Sunday and Monday were busy with local and long-distance day excursion traffic.

Sunday's programme commenced with the 9.30 am excursion from Exeter to Plymouth, which was joined at Newton Abbot by a portion from Paignton, arriving attached to the rear of a normal service train.

At 9.25 am an eight-coach train set forth from Cullompton, catering for passengers bound for Dawlish Warren, Dawlish and Teignmouth. This set of coaches spent the rest of the day shuttling between Newton Abbot and Exeter, augmenting the normal service, and finishing with two short evening trips from Dawlish Warren back to Exeter.

Also departing at 9.30 am for Paignton was an excursion from the Yeovil branch, starting from the ex-GWR Pen Mill station, and running via Yeovil Town to join the main line at Curry Rivel Junction.

Longer-distance excursions to Paignton, all starting at 9.10 am, came from Trowbridge, Paddington and Aberdare, arriving in front of the 8.45 am from Birmingham, which was not due to arrive in Paignton until 2.41 pm.

The return Birmingham and Aberdare trains did not leave Paignton until 8.25 pm and 9.05 pm respectively, so that their occupants can hardly have been home much before 2.30 am.

On Bank Holiday Monday the Plymouth Navy Days were a popular local outing and no fewer than four separate excursion trains were run from Torquay, Paignton, Exeter St David's and St Thomas, the latter going right through to Keyham, and another from Henbury, on the outskirts of Bristol.

In the opposite direction came excursions from Tavistock and Saltash to Goodrington Sands Halt, which was also the terminus for several of the regular local trains in the summer months.

Bridgwater residents had two excursion destinations to choose from on the Monday, and could go either to Paignton or to Exmouth, while passengers from Taunton were offered either Weymouth, via the Yeovil branch, or a trip to Seaton via the Chard branch.

The only long-distance excursion to Paignton on the Monday was from Kidderminster. During the Bank Holiday Monday afternoon and evening, as well as the returning excursions no fewer than six of the normal service trains were duplicated, thus completing a very busy weekend.

On branch lines such as the Moretonhampstead and Exe Valley, the normal two-coach trains were augmented to five or six coaches, and this picture shows a typical August Bank Holiday Monday crowd of the period waiting at West Exe Halt, on the outskirts of Tiverton, for the 9.25 am from Dulverton, behind 0-6-0T No 3659, which will take them as far as Exeter.

1 August 1987

Land of milk and 'Castles'

Caught in a flash of evening sunlight, which just reaches down into the closely trimmed cutting behind the Passage House Inn on the banks of the River Teign, 4-6-0 No 5098 *Clifford Castle* coasts into Newton Abbot with the Fridays-only 12.05 pm Paddington to Truro empty dining cars (see also page 58), as 2-8-0 No 3834 leaves for Kensington, West London, with the daily 12.20 pm up milk train from Penzance on 15 August 1958. *Clifford Castle* was the first of a new batch of 'Castle' Class engines to emerge from Swindon Works after the war, being released to traffic in May 1946. These engines were the first 'Castles' to have three-row superheaters, and the adoption of this higher degree of superheating meant that it was also necessary to change from the traditional GWR sight feed lubricator to a mechanical lubricator - this device can be seen mounted on the footplating between the curved steampipe and the leading splasher.

The name *Clifford Castle* was one of several 'Castle' names which had found considerable difficulty in maintaining their position over the centre splasher of one of the GWR's most numerous class of express passenger locomotives, before finally finding a permanent home on No 5098.

The first *Clifford Castle* was No 5046, one of 15 'Castles' turned out from Swindon during the spring and early summer of 1936. The name was, however, removed in August 1937, when it was decided to re-name over 20 'Castles' as 'Earls'. Apparently one of the members of the Upper House objected to finding that his title had been applied to a new class of GWR 4-4-0 for use on the Cambrian section, and felt he deserved something better, so No 5046 became *Earl Cawdor*.

The GWR, economical as ever, put back into the Swindon store the displaced 'Castle' nameplates, and they re-appeared on the 1938 batch of 'Castles', when *Clifford Castle* became No 5071.

However, war was approaching, and during the Battle of Britain in September 1940, with a quite uncharacteristic fit of popularist patriotism, though certainly catching the mood of the period, *Clifford Castle* again succumbed and No 5071 became *Spitfire*. During the next few months, 11 other 'Castle' names were replaced by those of aircraft familiar to everyone at that time.

The ability of the railway to carry liquid milk quickly and economically to the big city consumer was one of the early benefits the railway brought to the West Country. Traditionally, milk traffic on the railway was handled in 10-gallon churns carried in ventilated vans, which on the GWR were known as 'Siphons'. Long trainloads of these vans would carry the milk up to London every day. In the 1930s six-wheeled glass-lined tank wagons were introduced, each carrying up to 3,000 gallons of milk in bulk, and weighing 28 tons when full, nearly as much as a normal bogie passenger coach.

The 12.20 pm from Penzance to Kensington was the first of two milk trains which in 1958 travelled up to London each evening, and were often the heaviest trains of the day, weighing up to 550 tons. Running at passenger train speeds and usually hauled by one of the 4-6-0 classes - Laira is probably conserving its 4-6-0s for the Saturday passenger trains - the milk is being hauled by 2-8-0 No 3834, another engine with wartime connections. Built in 1941, it was originally part of a Government order for 60 of the class, but this order was cancelled after the fall of France in 1940.

8 August 1987

'Dukes' and 'Bulldogs'

The sight of this train, rolling into Newton Abbot under the old bowstring girder bridge and passing West signal box, will recall for some the halcyon pre-war years, when most of the GWR express passenger trains were piloted over the banks to Plymouth by 4-4-0s.

Although this scene has changed little since before the war, the waste ground behind the signal box, on which a row of cottages stood until demolished after the 1940 bombing raid on the town and station area, and the smokebox number plates on the engines, show this to be a 1950s picture, taken at 12.18 pm on 25 March 1954.

The train is the 8.00 am from Penzance to Paddington, hauled by 4-6-0 No 7031 *Cromwell's Castle*, and the occasion is the trial of 4-4-0 No 9023, one of the erstwhile 'Earl' Class 4-4-0s, on piloting duties similar to those performed first by 'Duke of Cornwall' and later by 'Bulldog' Class 4-4-0s in the years between the wars.

The trials lasted for several days, but the Newton Abbot and Laira men were not convinced that the 'Duke' boilers had the same free steaming qualities as those of the 'Bulldogs' they had been familiar with until 1948, and were reluctant to change back to what appeared to be a relic of the 19th century after several years of piloting with the much larger and more capable 'Manor' and 'Grange' Class 4-6-0s. The idea was therefore dropped and thereafter appearances by this 4-4-0 class in the West Country became a rarity.

A rather similar reaction was noted when these engines first appeared from Swindon in 1936, then numbered in the 32xx series, and named after Earls, although No 3201 retained the 'Duke' Class name *St Michael* for a time, before becoming *Earl of Dunraven*.

The class was intended as a replacement for the ageing 'Duke of Cornwall' Class 4-4-0s, then still needed on the lightly laid tracks of the Cambrian Division, on the lines to Aberystwyth and Pwllheli. The 'Duke of Cornwall' Class had first appeared in 1895, at a time when the elegant Dean 'Singles' were hauling the West Country expresses down to Exeter and Newton Abbot, but a stronger engine was needed for the rest of the journey over the Dartmoor foothills and on to Penzance.

In 1899 a variation of the 'Duke of Cornwall' Class appeared, which later became the heavier 'Bulldog' class, with the standard Swindon No 2 taper boiler, and these continued to be built up to 1910.

By 1936 many of the 'Dukes' were worn out, and as a lightweight engine was still required for the Cambrian and the Didcot, Newbury & Southampton lines, it was decided to marry the best of the 'Bulldog' frames and cylinders with the lighter, parallel, domed boilers of the 'Dukes', and so was produced the 'Earl' Class, or, as they later became known, the 'Dukedogs', after their mixed parentage.

This process ceased with the outbreak of war in 1939, and the 'Bulldogs' remaining in South Devon continued in daily use on local trains and piloting duties until 1948.

When the GWR era closed at the end of 1947, 11 'Bulldogs' were still allocated to Newton Abbot and Laira, among which were such well-remembered names as *Blasius*, *Dominion of Canada*, *Winnipeg*, *Vancouver*, *Madras* (see page 32), *Blackbird*, *Flamingo* and *Goldfinch*, the latter for ever immortalised by one Newton Abbot resident as *Goldfish*!

15 August 1987

Busy evening at Newton Abbot

This picture catches a busy moment at Newton Abbot, on Tuesday 6 August 1957 at 6.00 pm, with all three up roads and the bay platform in use.

Dominating the picture is the familiar outline of a '14xx' Class 0-4-2 tank. This one is No 1472, one of the final batch of five engines of this class turned out in April 1936. At that time numbered in the 48xx series, their numbers were required in 1946 for oil-burning 2-8-0 tender engines.

The oil-burning engines were eventually converted back to coal firing and reverted to their old numbers, but the '14xx' tanks kept their new numbers. This was in one way appropriate, because several batches of the '517' Class 0-4-2Ts, which the new engines were replacing during the 1930s, had also used the 14xx series of numbers.

No 1472's fireman has just regained the footplate after attaching the chain of the still dripping water crane bag to the post alongside the engine's buffer beam. The odd-looking object apparently sprouting out of the side of No 1472's smokebox is the chimney of the 'devil', a small stove found under each GWR water crane, lit during frosty weather to prevent it from freezing.

Having taken water, No 1472 will now run round her train, at present in the siding beyond the platform end, and then propel it back into the No 9 bay platform, where there will then be two trains, instead of the usual one. This is because it is Bank Holiday Week and the 4.25 pm Exeter to Heathfield auto-train via the Teign Valley line has been specially extended into Newton Abbot. This has been done with the object of avoiding overcrowding on the normally well-loaded 6.05 pm to Moretonhampstead, to be hauled by No 1472, which will then be followed out at 6.15 pm by the Teign Valley train, behind sister engine No 1468.

To the left of the picture can be seen the front end of 'Castle' Class 4-6-0 No 5053 *Earl Cairns*, which has brought up the 5.45 pm goods from Goodrington, bound for Hackney yard. This was a regular duty for the engine off the down 'Torbay Express' in 1957, though normally the engine was turned at Kingswear before coming back up the branch, and sometimes hauled the goods train while still carrying the 'Torbay Express' headboard.

In the background the first of the evening's three up Perishables trains has just arrived in platforms 7 and 8. This one is the 4.25 pm Plymouth Millbay to Paddington, hauled by train engine No 73029, one of the British Railways Standard Class '5' 4-6-0s then running on the Western Region. The pilot engine, 4-6-0 No 6938 *Corndean Hall*, whose fireman is emerging from the cab, tail-lamp in hand, is about to detach and proceed to shed via the turntable road.

The parcels train has a 23-minute scheduled stop at Newton Abbot, during which time the train engine with the empty gas tanks next to it - these are going up to Exeter for re-charging at the Gas Plant - will probably also detach to pick up the vans on the through road, before departing at 6.21 pm.

19 September 1987

Coombe Junction

This is the opposing view to that taken from this bridge on page 72, as we are now looking south towards Looe, with Lamellion Mill and Coombe Junction station in the foreground.

This picture was taken on the same morning as the previous one, 2 August 1958, and shows two trains crossing on the single track line from Liskeard to Looe. The train in the platform is the 8.40 am from Looe to Liskeard, headed by 2-6-2 tank No 4585, while the one just leaving in the distance, on the through line coming down under Lamellion bridge from Moorswater, is the 8.45 am from Liskeard to Looe, hauled by another engine of the same class.

Because of the difference in height between the Liskeard & Looe line on the valley floor and the Cornwall Railway main line across Liskeard and Moorswater viaducts, it was not until 1901 that a connection was established. By this time the GWR had already taken over the Cornwall Railway and within a few years, following some devious financial transactions by others on its behalf, the Liskeard & Looe Railway would be swallowed up too.

In the meanwhile, in order to obtain a reasonable gradient on the connecting line to the GWR, the junction was built facing towards Moorswater, and lies just out of sight beyond Coombe Junction signal box, giving rise to the curious anomaly that all trains between Liskeard and Looe have, to this day, to reverse direction at Coombe Junction.

With today's diesel units this is no great hardship, but in steam days the '45xx' tanks had to uncouple, pull forward to the buffer stops beneath the bridge, whistle as an indication to the signalman that it was safe to reverse the points, then run the length of the loop to beyond the signal box, whistle again, pick up the single line tablet from the signalman on the way back and couple up to the other end of the train. In addition, if this was the first of a pair of crossing trains, although the tablet would not be picked up until later, the driver would then pull out of the station beyond the signal box, before backing his train on to the right-hand track, ready to leave as soon as the other train was safely in the platform and the signalman had reversed the points and pulled off the signals.

This, then, is the situation before us. The 8.40 am from Looe has just arrived in the platform, and the fireman is down between the buffers uncoupling the engine from the train, while the signalman has already reversed the points and pulled off the signal for the 8.45 am from Liskeard to leave for Looe, and the train is already on the move.

During the afternoons of summer Saturdays, with the down trains often running unpredictably late, it was usual for the two branch trains to shuttle back and forth, connecting with the up trains and as many of the down trains as possible; this entailed some very smart work by the train crews.

Woe betide anyone in the vicinity of Coombe Junction looking for a quiet afternoon's snooze, as at intervals trains rattled into the station. The imperious Great Western whistle would echo sharply from the buildings, returning later from the distant hillside, while the engine's staccato exhaust beats would resemble machine-gun fire as it raced from one end of the station to the other.

Only after the train had rounded the hill, well on the way up to Liskeard, would peace return to the valley, occasionally to be broken by a distant rumble from the direction of Moorswater viaduct.

10 October 1987

Newton Abbot connection

The Great Western timetable for Summer 1938 advised the introduction of a new early morning service to London. This one was a real flyer, and must have demanded some very hard work by the locomotive fireman, if the advertised schedule was to be kept.

It left Plymouth North Rd at 7.20 am to arrive at Paddington at 11.50 am, and although $4^{1}/_{2}$ hours for this journey may not seem a very fast schedule, the intermediate stops at Taunton and Westbury made it a more demanding working than that of the celebrated 'Torbay Express'.

Both the main train from Plymouth and the branch portion, leaving Paignton at 7.50 am, were due to arrive at Newton Abbot at 8.10 am. This was unusual and may have been an example of the cosmetic adjustments sometimes applied to the public version of the railway timetables, unless the Paignton coaches were to be attached to the rear of the train, which would have been a reversal of the usual practice.

The normal procedure with trains joining at Newton Abbot was for the branch portion to arrive first, running through platform 8 - the one which has now become a car park - to stop at the far end of platform 7, so that the rear coach was well clear of the scissors crossover which divided the long outside face of the up island into two separate platforms. The engine which had brought this train up from Paignton would then detach, either to stable in the locomotive spur beyond the platform end, or to pull out beyond East signal box, before setting back across the main line to go to shed.

The main train from Plymouth, behind a 'King', 'Castle' or 'Star' Class engine, would normally arrive a few minutes later and stop, short of the scissors crossover, in platform 8. Its engine would also detach and proceed via the scissors crossover to the up through line, passing the Paignton portion, before setting back onto the front of it in platform 7.

Meanwhile, the station pilot engine will have attached itself to the rear of the Plymouth train and pushed it up to join the rear of the Paignton portion, as the shunter removes the blanking boards from the corridor connections and prepares to couple up.

Down on the track the Carriage & Wagon examiner will have been testing the carriage wheels with his long-handled hammer and feeling for any sign of an overheated axlebox, before the train resumes its fast run to London.

If everything has gone to plan, all this will have taken 5 minutes - much less time than it takes to write - and our train will be on its way at 8.15 am, stopping at Teignmouth and Dawlish, with a quick dash to Exeter, before a storming run over Whiteball summit on a 35-minute start-to-stop timing from Exeter to Taunton. With a schedule from Exeter to Paddington, including stops at Taunton and Westbury, which allows only 5 more minutes than that of the non-stop 'Torbay Express', the fireman on this train will, no doubt, be looking forward to the sight of Savernake station slipping past, where he will at last be able to put down his shovel and enjoy the downhill run into London, having already done his part in enabling the driver to record an on-time arrival at 11.50 am.

Our picture is not pre-war, but shows ex-GWR 4-6-0 No 6017 *King Edward* IV in the early British Railways blue livery, leaving platform 7 at Newton Abbot with the combined 3.55 pm Kingswear and 1.20 pm Penzance to Paddington train on 2 June 1952.

31 October 1987

On your marks . . .

Unofficial railway racing has always been discouraged, the more so after local railway managements learned their lesson the hard way in the early years of this century, when the semi-official racing between the Great Western and the London & South Western Railways on the 'Ocean Liner' specials between Plymouth and London had led eventually to the disastrous high-speed derailment of an LSWR train at Salisbury in 1906.

No such problems were likely to occur on the short stretch between Newton Abbot and Aller Junction, where our picture shows ex-GWR 4-6-0 No 4936 *Kinlet Hall* overtaking British Railways 'Britannia' Class 4-6-2 No 70019 *Lightning* on train 100, the legendary 5.30 am from Paddington to Penzance via Bristol, on 12 November 1955.

Picture Newton Abbot station on a summer evening in 1944, grimy and war damaged, with a constant procession of freight, Perishables and Parcels trains trundling through. Down the main line comes the 7.10 pm stopping train from Exeter to Plymouth, at its head Southern Railway 'N' Class 2-6-0 No 1409, which grinds to a halt in platform 4 as doors swing open and weary workers spill out on to the platform, making either for the stairs or for the Paignton train waiting at platform 2, at its head Great Western 2-6-2T No 4516.

Both trains are due to leave Newton Abbot at 8.05 pm, but it is 8.06 pm before the guard of the Plymouth train can swing shut the heavy van doors, as the porters pull a barrow-load of parcels across to our Paignton train.

Assisted by the guard, the parcels are soon loaded into our train and all seems set for a good race, as the Southern engine whistles and sets forth, plodding out past West box with that slight slap in the motion typical of the class and so rarely heard from the Great Western engines. At that moment a late passenger comes running down the stairs. Willing hands bundle him into our compartment and slam the door, the guard waves his flag and we are off. But by now the other train has not only passed West box, but is out of sight under the road bridge and almost all thought of a race has gone. Almost, but not quite all, because we know our driver to be Bill Bishop, one of a group known affectionately as 'the old men', who has stayed on for the duration and is a noted hard runner. No 4516 is also one of the best of the Newton '45s', and the combination produces a start worthy of any racehorse.

With the lever well forward and the regulator wide open, we take off down the platform, clattering and crashing over the crossings and under the road bridge. Rarely has a Newton '45' been asked to perform as 4516 did that evening.

As we come round the corner the other train can be seen still plodding across the Decoy embankment, but we are fast overtaking it. Our speed rises to 40 mph, the wheels of the '45' just a blur and the exhaust a roar. Perhaps 50 mph is reached, fully 15 mph more than the Plymouth train.

As we come on to the final straight beside the main road and surge past the Plymouth train, startled looks come from the passengers, and no less surprised are the Southern crew on No 1409 as our last coach sweeps past them, with appropriate gestures from the last compartment.

At Aller box the lines part company and the race is over, but whatever the start-to-pass record was from Newton to Aller, Bill Bishop and No 4516 broke it that evening in 1944.

12 December 1987

Brampford Speke

Travellers on the main line between Exeter and Stoke Canon, where the Exe Valley line left the main line, will be familiar with the flooded fields that border the railway line when the River Exe is in spate.

Bearing away to the left, immediately after passing the now closed Stoke Canon station, is the formation which once carried the Exe Valley line, distinguishable these days only by a single remaining railway fence. This was, until 1963, the direct rail link between Tiverton and Exeter, and the first station on the line took the name of the village of Brampford Speke, which stood safely on higher ground overlooking the flood plain, less than a mile from Stoke Canon. This picture was taken on 9 December 1961 and shows ex-GWR 0-4-2 tank No 1471 propelling the 1.55 pm from Dulverton via Tiverton to Exeter train away from Brampford Speke, across the water meadows which separated the railway from the village.

The only access to Brampford Speke station was by footbridge across the river Exe, and because of this disadvantage the station never possessed any goods facilities. However, when it opened, with the railway, in May 1885, Brampford Speke was a full station with a Station Master who was provided with a house alongside the station, and two porter-signalmen. But by 1907 the signal box had been closed, and the station itself was closed for a time during the First World War,

at the outbreak of which the Station Master's annual salary had been £70.

The station might have been remarkably short-lived if a proposal by the GWR early in 1892 had been carried through. In that year the GWR decided to re-site the old Stoke Canon station from a position by the road crossing to the north of the junction with the Exe Valley line, to a position on the junction, and it was their announced intention to close Brampford Speke when this work was completed in 1894. However, the villagers protested against their enforced winter walk through the flooded fields to Stoke Canon and the GWR relented.

With its isolated location and with only the traffic of a small village to sustain it, the station was demoted to halt status in 1923. The station buildings were closed, later to be sold for domestic use, and the villagers had to make do with an unheated hut in which to wait for their trains for the remaining 40 years, until the passenger service was withdrawn in October 1963.

The train in our picture is typical of those used on the Exe Valley line in its latter years - an auto-train - capable of working in either direction with the engine either pulling or, as in this case, pushing, and often referred to as a push-pull train.

23 January 1988

Dawlish Warren

One of the most popular venues for a day's outing from Exeter and the whole of the Exe valley area was, and to a lesser extent still is, Dawlish Warren. With its extensive beach facilities, golf course and other amusements, Dawlish Warren has attracted thousands of day-trippers over the years since the Great Western Railway first gave the general public quick and easy access to this part of the coastline by opening the Warren Halt on 1 July 1905. This was one of the many Halts opened during the early years of the century to augment the existing pattern of stations, and the popularity of this one was such that by 1911 it was re-named Dawlish Warren with the status of a full station. At that time the platforms were located 17 chains south of the present station site, close to the still existing footbridge across the line.

The present station with its four-track layout was opened on 23 September 1912 and included long running loops on both up and down roads, where slow-moving loose-coupled goods trains could be stopped to be overtaken by other traffic. In addition to the engine and brake-van, these loops could hold trains of up to 75 wagons in length.

This picture, taken on 29 July 1961, shows the massive bulk of ex-GWR express freight 2-8-0 No 4707 drawing into Dawlish Warren station with the 13 coaches of the 7.30 am from Paddington to Kingswear.

This was one of several expresses which called at Dawlish Warren on summer Saturdays to provide a service for local day-trippers and for people arriving on holiday, at a period of the day when the density of long-distance trains prevented the insertion of any local trains into the timetable between Exeter and Newton Abbot. Long-distance passengers on the following 6.40 am from Leicester to Paignton, which was that day double-headed by ex-GWR 4-6-0s Nos 4985 *Allesley Hall* and 6874 *Haughton Grange*, were scheduled for a stop at Exeter St Thomas to pick up returning Saturday morning commuters, as well as a call at Dawlish Warren. Later that afternoon, passengers on the 9.05 am Liverpool to Plymouth, the second of two Liverpool expresses, both of which stopped at Dawlish Warren, will have been even less pleased to find that their train was being used to convey the afternoon commuters to their homes, and called at all stations from Exeter to Newton Abbot except Exminster.

On Saturdays at that time Exminster station was served only by down trains in the early morning and by up trains in the evening - passengers wishing to travel up the line and return the same day were not catered for, all part of the pre-closure ritual of those days, although it must be said that a slightly better service was provided on weekdays.

The footbridge at Dawlish Warren, from which this picture was taken, was demolished a few years ago, but the central portion was re-used and now spans the Paignton branch, carrying the path which leads from the Newton Road to Edginswell, just north of the Hamelin Way roundabout.

6 February 1988

'The Line to Legend Land'

While browsing through a catalogue of second-hand railway books which dropped through my letter-box recently - one of the few attractive items of unsolicited mail to arrive - I was intrigued by the quantity of official GWR publications offered, which far exceeded that of all the other railway companies put together. Most readers who had any interest in the GWR during the inter-war years will be familiar with the series of 1 shilling volumes for 'boys of all ages' produced by the company and bearing such titles as *Locos of the Royal Road*, *Track Topics* or *Cheltenham Flyer*. All were written by W. G. Chapman and the series had commenced in 1923 with *The 10.30 Limited*, followed in 1924 by *Caerphilly Castle*.

Each milestone in the progress of the GWR was celebrated with another volume in the series, so that the introduction of the 'King' Class 4-6-0s in 1927 was followed next year by a volume entitled *The King of Railway Locomotives*.

But probably the most familiar GWR publication to be seen by the general public was the annual edition of *Holiday Haunts*. Before the days of package holidays, when travel agents were used only by the rich to book cruises, or long holidays in South Africa using the weekly sailings of the Union Castle steamers, the average person who could afford a holiday and fancied somewhere on the GWR system bought a copy of *Holiday Haunts* and from its hundreds of pages selected their landlady or small hotel.

Although the 1920s and 1930s were the period which saw the greatest activity by the GWR Publicity Department, *Holiday Haunts* had been published at least since the early years of this century. Even in 1894 the GWR was seeking to attract American tourists, who in those days would mainly have arrived at Liverpool, with an *Illustrated Guide to the Great Western Railway of England*.

By 1911 the company had recognised the interest people outside the railway had in its locomotives and published the first edition of a paperback booklet which was to become one of their best-sellers. Originally titled *Names of Engines*, it later became *GWR Engines - Names, Numbers, Types and Classes* and introduced many a youngster to the GWR's principal locomotive classes. It had reached its 14th edition by 1938, with further editions to follow after the war.

In addition, the GWR produced many books about the area it served, with romantic titles such as *North Wales*, *The British Tyrol*, *The Line to Legend Land* and *Wessex White Horses and Other Turf Landmarks on the GWR*.

But perhaps the best-loved of the GWR productions were the magnificent three-ply wooden jigsaw puzzles. Ideal for passing a winter evening in those pre-television days, each came in a deep ribbon-tied rectangular box, and included a map of the GWR system. The jigsaw 'Royal Route to the West' depicted a scene in the Dartmoor foothills not dissimilar from this picture, which shows ex-GWR 4-6-0 No 6015 *King Richard III* racing down Rattery bank towards Totnes on 11 October 1959 with the Sunday 10.10 am from Plymouth to Paddington.

13 February 1988

Bristol goods (1)

On a frosty morning towards the end of October 1955, 4-6-0 No 6996 *Blackwell Hall* comes storming up the bank past Stoneycombe with the 2.25 am goods train from Bristol bound for Tavistock Junction yard, outside Plymouth.

The crisp bark from her exhaust - always the sign of a true Swindon product, where the craft of valve setting was regarded as something of a mystical art - echoes back from the quarry face as the wagons rattle past.

Blackwell Hall was then not quite seven years old, having been turned out from Swindon in January 1949, two years after nationalisation, but built to the GWR 'Modified Hall' design of 1944.

The 'Modified Halls' were readily distinguishable from the bulk of the 'Hall' Class by their larger steam pipes, joining the cylinders to the smokebox, and by their continuous plate-frames which extended through to the buffer beam, and plate-frame bogies.

Within 12 months Swindon would again be painting the 'Halls' in a lined green livery very similar to that carried before the war, but in 1955 *Blackwell Hall* was still in the British Railways standard black livery for mixed traffic locomotives, lined out in red, cream and grey. When clean this looked very smart, but although the lining is visible in this picture, the engine and tender are covered in a layer of dust and soot, which soften the effect this livery made when really clean.

The pace of the average goods train in those days was steady rather than fast, this one taking an hour to reach Bridgwater, its first stop where 20 minutes were allowed for traffic to be detached.

At Taunton there was a brief 5-minute pause for a change of crew before leaving for Victory siding, between Norton Fitzwarren and Wellington, where a 50-minute rest was scheduled to allow other trains to pass, including the 11.50 pm Paddington to Penzance night sleeper.

At 5.20 am the train left Victory siding, stopping briefly at Wellington to attach the banker, before climbing to Whiteball summit, which it was due to pass at 5.51 am. A further 58 minutes were absorbed at Tiverton Junction where further loaded wagons were shunted and left, either for unloading or to join the branch goods to Tiverton or to Hemyock.

At Exeter the train was due to be examined before proceeding on to Dawlish Warren, where it went into the loop to allow the 6.25 am Bristol to Plymouth to overtake. Hackney sidings, outside Newton Abbot, were reached at 9.19 am and here there was a lengthy wait, possibly while the train engine went off to shed to be replaced by a fresh engine, before the journey was resumed at 10.45 am.

At Aller Junction the signalman will have put this train into the loop, to allow the banking engine to be attached at the rear. Then, after the signalman has lowered the loop exit signal and the engines have exchanged crow whistles, together they will set forth towards Dainton tunnel.

This was just one of many goods trains that day, in an era when the railway was principally engaged in transporting the nation's freight and the passengers were merely the icing on a very large cake of goods trains.

Overleaf we'll have a look at the rear of this train.

20 February 1988

Bristol goods (2)

Here we see the brake-van and the banking engine on the rear of 2.25 am goods train from Bristol to Tavistock Junction, on 29 October 1955, pictured on the previous page. Helping 4-6-0 No 6996 *Blackwell Hall* and approaching Stoneycombe at the rear is ex-GWR 2-6-2 tank No 5158, one of the fleet of 'Large Prairie' tanks kept at Newton Abbot principally for banking duties at Aller and Totnes. But they were also used on passenger and goods workings between Exeter and Kingswear, for piloting passenger trains between Newton Abbot and either Brent or Plymouth, and during the last years of its passenger service they were also seen on the Moretonhampstead branch.

There were usually nine of this class at Newton Abbot, though the number varied slightly from year to year and, despite attempts to introduce other classes for banking, the '51xx' tanks remained the preferred engines for this job until the end of the steam era.

Although this particular engine, No 5158, was one of a batch not built until 1930, the basic design was that of Mr G. J. Churchward's prototype for the class which emerged from Swindon Works in 1903, bearing the number 99. This was one of several prototype engines produced at that time by Mr Churchward and intended to cover the needs of the GWR for the next 20 years.

In fact, these standard designs, as slightly modified by his successor Mr C. B. Collett, were sufficiently in advance of their time to see out the life of the company. As with so many of the engines built by British Railways, both steam and diesel, the final examples of this class built in 1949 had very short lives, some lasting less than 11 years, before being replaced by the diesel multiple units.

In 1955 No 5158 was in the plainest of the five liveries it carried during its life, British Railways black, relieved only by the copper cap chimney and the 'lion and wheel' emblem on the tankside.

Next to the engine is a typical Great Western 20-ton brake-van. These are often referred to nowadays as 'Toads', which was the GWR's telegraphic description of these vehicles. In pre-war years this brake-van would have been branded with the name of its home depot between the large letters 'G' and 'W' in the end panels, and also possibly branded with a specific working.

Then, during the war, most of the brake-vans became common user and regular workings were a thing of the past, and vans from the most remote corners of the GWR system could be seen outside the Newton Abbot Carriage & Wagon Works awaiting repairs. Among those noted at the time were brake-vans branded NEATH, from South Wales; OXLEY SIDINGS (Wolverhampton); WEYMOUTH; LUDLOW, Shropshire; RUABON, near Wrexham; and FERNDALE in the upper reaches of the Rhondda Valley. Apart from the van from Oxley Sidings, it is unlikely that any of these would have had regular workings through Newton Abbot before the war.

British Railways did not go beyond branding vans in regular use as 'Not in Common Use', as with the van in our picture, and the Great Western 'Toads' continued to be anonymous to the end of their days.

27 February 1988

Lineside chores

On 11 March 1960 a 'Hall' Class 4-6-0 slogs up to the summit at Dainton tunnel in a stiff easterly breeze that sends the exhaust steam billowing through the farm orchard across the tracks.

In the foreground a member of the permanent way gang responsible for this length of the line is engaged in repairing the railway fence, re-stringing the wires of the typically Great Western post-and-wire fencing. Originally constructed of wooden posts supported at either end by sawn-up lengths of used broad gauge 'bridge rail', the fence now has a number of concrete posts included in its length, doubtless inserted where the old wooden posts have succumbed to one of the numerous lineside fires that could be started by red-hot cinders lifted from the firebox and thrown high into the sky by the exhaust of labouring steam engines on this section; this despite the constant attention given to cutting back the lineside vegetation, right back to the railway fence, which gave the railways of those days such a tidy appearance. From mid-summer onwards each year, the sub-ganger and his lengthmen would be found hand-scything the embankment and cutting sides - a thankless, not to say thirst-making, task on a July day - and later controlling the burning of the cut grass.

This regular cutting and burning produced an ideal habitat for the spring wild flowers, which blossomed in profusion on the lineside, and, later in the season, for the wild strawberries that often provided a welcome addition to the lineside photographer's lunchtime sandwiches.

The Kingsbridge branch was particularly notable for its spring display of primroses and had British Railways not been in such an all-fired hurry to dismantle the line after it closed, letting the demolition contract while preservation proposals were being initiated, this line would certainly today have been known as 'The Primrose Line'.

Sadly, with the demise of the steam engine and the consequent lessening of the fire risk, British Railways has in many areas allowed its previously tidy and well-kept lineside banks to grow unchecked. One result of this inattention and the passage of the years has been found in the Southern Region, which has recently suffered from an increasing incidence of wheelslip problems due to the leaf fall from the trees and bushes it had itself allowed to grow beside the line, forming a greasy mush on the rails.

However, to return to the picture, the engine hauling this train is 4-6-0 No 6959 *Peatling Hall*, the prototype engine of the 'Modified Hall' Class. Along with all the other 'Halls' built during the war after February 1941, she was originally nameless and carried only the identifying words 'Hall class' painted on the centre splashers.

The standard GWR nameplate consists of brass letters riveted to a steel plate with a brass border. The amount of brass used being minimal, the omission of nameplates during the war was rather more of a gesture towards the general war effort than an action calculated to advance the overthrow of Hitler; nevertheless No 6959 did not acquire her name until December 1946, over 12 months after the war's end.

5 March 1988

Westwood

Of the many pictures that I took in Cornwall during the late 1950s and early 1960s this has always been one of my favourites, not least because it captured for all time a view of the long-abandoned Westwood signal box, situated in an extremely isolated position high above the Glyn Valley between St Pinnock and Westwood viaducts on the Cornish main line almost exactly 1 mile west of Doublebois station.

Doublebois station lay at the summit of the 6-mile climb from Bodmin Road facing eastbound trains coming out of Cornwall. The heavy summer Saturday trains of those days, rarely less than 12 and sometimes up to 15 coaches in length, needed two engines if even a reasonable rate of progress was to be maintained up this bank.

Travelling today by train through Cornwall one hardly notices these banks, but in steam days they were formidable obstacles to progress and speed could drop almost to walking pace on occasions, although 15-20 mph would be more usual - time enough to enjoy the views from the many high viaducts on this section.

Although this was 2 August 1958, the weather was decidedly stormy and a westerly gale was following the train up the bank and almost pushing the steam ahead of it and through the wooded hillside behind the signal box.

The signal standing at danger is the Largin down distant, controlled by Largin signal box, about three-quarters of a mile down the line beyond St Pinnock and Largin viaducts. The train is the 12-coach 9.20 am Saturdays-only from St Ives to Paddington, effectively a part of the 'Cornish Riviera Express', and is already almost 2 hours into its journey, hauled by loco-motives of two classes well suited to the undulating Cornish main line.

In front is the imposing outline of 4-6-0 No 1021 *County of Montgomery*, still with its original single chimney; in later years the class were disfigured by the replacement of the single chimney by a very short double chimney, which, whatever it may have done for the steaming qualities of the boiler, completed ruined the engines' appearance.

Behind, and barely visible through the steam being blown down over it, is 4-6-0 No 6808 *Beenham Grange*, once a Newton Abbot engine and a member of the very popular 'Grange' Class, which always performed well in Cornwall.

Westwood box was a typical Cornwall Railway signal box, built of local stone with a slate roof surmounted by a finial. It was square in plan and originally had windows facing the track and on each side, now long since boarded up. It was built around 1874 when Westwood quarry was opened up to supply the railway with ballast stone and also with stone for rebuilding the original Brunel timber viaducts, to enable the single broad gauge line to be replaced by a double line after the broad gauge was abandoned in 1892.

It had closed by 1893 when this task was completed and was probably used thereafter as a refuge and store for men working on the track. Sadly it was demolished in the early 1960s, thereby severing yet another link with the early days on the Cornwall Railway, which was not taken over by the GWR until 1889.

16 April 1988

Christow

On a beautiful summer's evening in August 1953, two trains cross at Christow on the Teign Valley line. A lady passenger makes her way to the boarded crossing, ready to go across the lines once the train running in from Exeter has cleared it. At Christow, as at most stations, large cast iron notices were prominently displayed at the platform ends requesting passengers to cross the lines by the footbridge, but at country stations these were often ignored if the footbridge was inconveniently distant.

The boarded crossing was installed for the use of the staff, particularly to enable them to get the wheeled luggage barrows across the tracks, either of the two-wheeled variety for a few parcels or a passenger's luggage, or the typical GWR four-wheeled steerable flat barrow on which a whole mountain of parcels could be carried - provided there were enough staff available to push it up the platform ramp.

By 1953 Christow was coming to the close of its days as a busy country station. It had opened to passengers on 1 July 1903, when the Exeter Railway completed its line from City Basin Junction, just south of Exeter St Thomas station, through to Christow.

Here the Exeter Railway made an end-on junction with a long siding from the original Teign Valley line which had been opened to passengers from Heathfield to Ashton 21 years earlier, in 1882.

So, now for the first time not only was there a direct rail service from Exeter to the Teign Valley, with its valuable mineral deposits, but the GWR also had the use of an alternative inland route if a landslide or washout was to shut the coastal line. The promoters of the Exeter Railway, originally the Exeter, Teign Valley & Chagford Railway, grossly exaggerated the traffic potential of the line to potential shareholders by assuming that the GWR would send its special through fish, perishable and excursion trains over the line to avoid the then single-line bottleneck at Dawlish.

However, the GWR was already planning the completion of its double-track line to Plymouth and the Exeter Railway became a relatively peaceful country feeder to the main line.

With the completion of the through line and the building of Christow station, the latter then became the railhead for the mineral traffic, and the buildings associated with this can be seen in the background of the picture.

The stone from the Scatter Rock Quarry came to Christow by aerial ropeway until 1950, when the quarry closed, but traffic from the Bridford Barytes Mine continued until 1953, arriving by road lorry for tipping into rail wagons.

The original long siding continued west out of Christow goods yard across river and road to the Devon Basalt and Granite Co's mine, but this had closed by 1931, and in the immediate pre-war years I recall that this part of the yard was yielding vast quantities of luscious blackberries.

On this summer evening, well before the closure of the line was envisaged, we are standing beside 0-4-2T No 1469 on the 6.20 pm from Heathfield to Exeter, while running in on the other track is 0-6-0T No 7716 on the 6.05 pm from Exeter. Both the trailers which make up this train, Nos 148 and 215, are conversions from steam railmotors, the first being of the suburban type with entrances at either end, and the second of the branch-line type with a centre entrance. The latter may well have worked over this line before conversion, as steam railmotors worked much of the passenger service for many years.

23 April 1988

Brent

As the down 'Cornishman' express from Wolverhampton to Penzance sweeps through Brent station behind 'Castle' Class 4-6-0 No 5085 *Evesham Abbey* on 26 March 1960, the passengers get but a fleeting glimpse of this junction station for the Kingsbridge line.

We, however, can take a longer look at a scene, so soon to be swept away but in 1960 almost unchanged from the day that the Kingsbridge branch opened on 19 December 1893. The main line itself in this area had only been doubled since May 1893, so from being a quiet village station with a passing loop on a single-line railway at the beginning of the year, by Christmas 1893 Brent had become a double-track main-line station with branch trains coming and going to Kingsbridge.

Brent had achieved a certain notoriety in 1891, when the down 'Zulu', the unofficial name given to the 3.00 pm express from Paddington, became snowed up in the station during a great blizzard on Monday 9 March. The train had already been delayed for nearly 3 hours at Rattery signal box, where the single-line section then commenced, while the driver had taken the engine forward to check that the line was passable to Brent, the normal box-to-box telegraph lines having been brought down by the snow.

The train was eventually hauled into Brent at about 11.00 pm, but progress beyond this point was by now impossible.

There was, of course, no refreshment room at Brent and the 40 passengers on the train, who had expected to be at their destination by suppertime, were not prepared for what turned out to be a four-day stay in Brent.

They complained afterwards that the Brent village traders had raised their prices to 'famine level' when they attempted to buy some supplies next morning, one gentleman having to pay 6 shillings for a bottle of brandy! However, they were befriended by the villagers themselves and were also very appreciative of the railway staff, including the driver and fireman who managed to keep the fire going on the engine throughout their ordeal. In this the crew were assisted by several soldiers and sailors on the train, who helped with the arduous task of feeding the engine's tanks with snow, because the water crane at the end of the platform was frozen solid.

By the time the line ahead had been cleared, which was not until Friday 13 March, several of the passengers had made their escape, presumably those who could either afford the cost of horses, or who were prepared to walk through the snowdrifts to their destination, so that only about 20 passengers remained with the train when it eventually pulled into Plymouth four days late.

However, to return to our 1960 scene, it is remarkable how little change there had been since a very similar view taken in 1910. In 1960 the station was still gas-lit, and the track layout and buildings are identical to those in the earlier view. Even the Permanent Way Department's little store of equipment in the right foreground was there in 1910 - spare sections of rail, sleepers and chairs, together with a demountable four-wheeled flatbed trolley for getting the materials to the spot where they were needed.

But all was soon to change. By September 1963 the Kingsbridge branch had closed and just over a year later the Brent station of 1893 had also closed its doors for the last time.

7 May 1988

Train numbers

Then 35 years young, ex-GWR 2-6-0 No 6351 sails through the Powderham reverse curves between Exminster and Starcross on 26 July 1958 with the down 'Devonian' express, the 9.05 am from Bradford to Paignton.

This was a lucky shot if ever there was one, as the tail end of an up empty stock train has only just cleared in time to allow us to see this recently ex-Works 'Mogul' emerge into the evening sunlight. Resplendent in the still spotless lined green livery into which the class was then being repainted, No 6351 makes a fine sight as she steams along the banks of the River Exe towards Starcross.

Even in 1958 it was unusual to see a 'Mogul' at the head of a named train in this area, though this one is not carrying the official headboard which would normally have been carried on the top lamp bracket. Instead it has the rather insignificant Midland Region style of train reporting number on the top lamp bracket above the smokebox number plate, which was another Midland innovation, also brought into use on ex-GWR engines by British Railways.

The disadvantage with the Midland style of train reporting numbers, which comprised paper numbers - in this case 444 - pasted on to a wooden board, was that on wet days they tended to either get peeled back, or wash off altogether, so trains could arrive in South Devon with only one or two of the three figures still visible, or on particularly wet days, with just a blank board!

The GWR style of train reporting numbers consisted of large painted metal plates set in a frame mounted on the centre of the smokebox door, rather ungainly but visible from a long distance, which was, after all, the object of the exercise. One snag with these was that sometimes the shed staff found themselves short of a particular number and had to resort to adapting one white-painted number to another using white chalk. The figure 3, for example, could easily be made into an 8, or a 1 into a 4, but these alterations could also get washed off in the rain. A fairly recent example of this was the steam special run in connection with the 'GW150' celebrations at Easter 1985. This train left Bristol behind 4-6-0s Nos 6000 *King George V* and 7819 *Hinton Manor* bearing the GWR-style train reporting number 122. However, after running through very heavy rain in the Taunton area, when the train was next seen at Cullompton the reporting number had become 1 blank 2 - evidently the middle number had been chalked on and not painted.

Finally, to return to the picture, to the left of the departing empty stock train stands the up distant signal controlled by Powderham signal box. This was one of two boxes - the other was Cotfield - opened in 1924 to increase the line capacity by breaking up the long sections between Starcross, Exminster and Exeter City Basin.

Both lines have recently been relaid with the latest heavy section flat-bottomed rail to replace the old bullhead-section chaired track, but still laid in 60-foot lengths so the passengers still have the comforting 'clickity clack' of the wheels passing over the rail joints to lull them to sleep. Why anyone should want to go to sleep on a train journey I cannot imagine . . .

28 May 1988

Summer Saturday at Whiteball (1)

It is one of life's little ironies that in order to take photographs of trains from the lineside, it is in most cases necessary to travel by road to reach the desired spot. And travelling by car on a peak summer Saturday in the late 1950s was purgatory - fortunately I had a motor cycle, or most of the pictures in this book would not have been taken.

Nevertheless, even on a motor cycle it still took $2^1/2$ hours to reach the Devon/Somerset border safely from Torquay, along the snaking single carriageway that was then the main road to Exeter and all points east.

The A38, still virtually unchanged since before the war, was joined at the T-junction at the foot of Telegraph Hill, which really was then a fearsomely steep gradient. Overtaking on the way thousands of stationary cars, which by mid-morning could stretch from Kingsteignton to the far end of the Exeter bypass - in those days far more notorious for traffic hold-ups then the M25 is today - one joined the slow-moving line of cars and coaches leaving the county via the main street of Cullompton and over the Blackdown Hills.

This was not a road journey to be undertaken lightly, and I did not usually venture this far east by road more than once during the peak season, but on Saturday 26 July 1958 I decided to fight my way through the traffic and eventually turned off the A38 into a quiet country lane leading down to the lineside, at the Taunton end of Whiteball tunnel.

Officially this location should be described as Milepost $172^3/4$, the mileage from Paddington over the original route via Bristol. Within sight of the eastern portal of the tunnel, it was an ideal spot from which to both observe and photograph.

It provided a nice contrast - westbound trains labouring up the 1 in 80 gradient to the tunnel mouth, where the gradient eased slightly to 1 in 128 for the 1,092 yards to the Devon portal, while eastbound trains had the advantage of the falling gradient through the tunnel to gather speed and burst out at full pelt, many with a non-stop run to Paddington then in prospect.

This picture sets the scene admirably, with ex-GWR 4-6-0 No 6831 *Bearley Grange* pulling slowly towards the tunnel with the 10.15 am train from Paddington to Kingswear, as ex-GWR 4-6-0 No 5066 *Wardour Castle* bursts forth with the 11.15 am from Plymouth North Road to Paddington on 26 July 1958.

The completion of Whiteball tunnel had delayed the opening of the Bristol & Exeter Railway to Exeter for 12 months. From May 1843 to May 1844 trains from Bristol had terminated at a temporary station at Beam Bridge, where the turnpike road - later to be the A38 - crossed the railway, about 1 mile in the Taunton direction.

Whiteball tunnel was dug from both ends and from 14 vertical shafts, the extreme depth of which below the Blackdown Hills was almost 200 feet; these were filled in after completion of the tunnel. It is straight except at the Somerset end - at which we are looking - where the first 66 yards are on a 68-chain radius curve. Because of the unstable nature of the ground through which it was driven, the tunnel is brick-lined throughout, in places to a thickness of up to 2 ft 10 in, and never less than 2 feet.

4 June 1988

Summer Saturday at Whiteball (2)

It was nearly mid-day before I eventually arrived at the Whiteball lineside on 26 July 1958, near the summit of the main line between Taunton and Exeter. Already the morning flow of trains into the West Country was well under way, the first one seen being the 7.05 am from Paddington to Penzance behind 4-6-0 No 4979 *Wootton Hall* only 44 minutes late, which was quite creditable for this peak Saturday for down traffic at the start of the Midlands Holiday Fortnight, when almost all manufacturing industry in the area closed down at the start of the school holidays.

On that Saturday morning, between midnight and 7.00 am, over 45 trains would have passed over Whiteball summit, the earliest heading for Penzance and Newquay, but just on a half going to Torquay and Paignton, with the first of these due to arrive at 2.50 am.

Unfortunately, the timetable planners assumed a headway of 6 minutes for trains to follow each other over Whiteball summit, but in practice this was rarely achievable, and out of the 36 trains that passed me that afternoon only three managed to achieve or better this standard.

Consequently, on this peak weekend, the night trains tended to run very late and this sometimes reacted on the earliest of the Saturday morning departures. It should be remembered that the average train in those days was 12 coaches in length, with a normal maximum of 14 coaches in the down direction, so that some of the locomotives provided to haul them were approaching their maximum capacity when faced with the climb up to Whiteball summit.

To provide assistance to any that might need it, banking engines were provided at Wellington, and on this particular afternoon 'Large Prairie' 2-6-2Ts Nos 4128, 5172 and 5185 were on duty.

Altogether nine trains stopped at Wellington for a banker during the afternoon, and during one remarkable period of 22 minutes, from 2.40 pm to 3.02 pm, all three bankers were in use assisting 14-coach trains.

The only trains to beat the 6-minute barrier were the first part of the 6.55 am from Wolverhampton to Paignton, loaded to 12 coaches behind 4-6-0 No 6978 *Haroldstone Hall* - a very good performance this; the 13-coach 9.05 am from Swansea to Kingswear, which was double-headed by 4-6-0s Nos 5915 *Trentham Hall* and 4914 *Cranmore Hall* and so had an unfair advantage; and the 8.00 am Sheffield to Kingswear, loaded to 14 coaches behind 4-6-0 No 5969 *Honington Hall*, which had the help of 2-6-2T No 5172 at the rear.

As might be expected of the premier train on the line, both parts of the 'Cornish Riviera Limited' came up the bank in fine style. The main train, seen in our picture, was behind 4-6-0 No 6021 *King Richard II*, whose fireman appears to be supplying more steam than the driver can use, despite the 14-coach load behind the tender. The second part, also with 14 coaches, came up behind 4-6-0 No 6013 *King Henry VIII*.

Only one engine appeared to be in any trouble, and this was later in the afternoon, when a heavy drizzle had set in, and 4-6-0 No 6915 *Mursley Hall* had difficulty keeping her feet on the wet rail with the 13-coach 8.00 am from Manchester to Penzance.

A comparison with today's timetable shows that there are now only eight overnight trains compared with up to 45 that ran in 1958, and during the period that 36 down day trains ran in 1958, there are now only 17 trains. This gives some indication of the transfer of holiday traffic from rail to road that has occurred since the building of the motorways.

11 June 1988

Summer Saturday at Whiteball (3)

Concluding our look at the flow of trains over Whiteball summit during the afternoon of 26 July 1958, and following our examination of the down line traffic, it is now time to look at the up trains.

Generally speaking the up trains have a much easier run up the Exe and Culm valleys, and although the gradient gradually steepens towards the summit, it is nowhere more than 1 in 115, and after a climb up from Cullompton to Tiverton Junction there is even a short downhill stretch on which to recover, before the final 4 miles through Sampford Peverell (now Tiverton Parkway) and Burlescombe up to the summit near Whiteball Siding signal box.

No assistance by way of banking engines was provided on the run up from Exeter, and although in the early 1900s it was quite common for the heavier trains to be double-headed from Exeter up to Whiteball summit, this practice died out when the more powerful GWR 4-6-0s became available for all the heavy trains. Average speeds over the summit were quite low by today's standards, and a 'King' or 'Castle' Class 4-6-0 with a full load would be unlikely to top the bank at more than 40 mph, even if given a clear road all the way up.

On this Saturday, early indications were of trouble somewhere on the Kingswear branch - probably a severe bout of stock indigestion at Paignton - as the 10.30 am from Torquay to Paddington, loaded to 12 coaches behind 4-6-0 No 5043 *Earl of Mount Edgcumbe*, came up 28 minutes late, following the 10.10 am from Paignton to Cardiff hauled by 4-6-0 No 1024 *County of Pembroke*, which it should have preceded from Exeter.

Subsequent trains starting from Paignton or Torquay that morning were up to 45 minutes late passing Whiteball, but it was noticeable that the Kingswear departures such as the 13-coach 'Torbay Express' behind 4-6-0 No 7001 *Sir James Milne* kept much better time.

The early Plymouth and Cornwall trains were keeping good time that afternoon, including the 14-coach up 'Cornish Riviera Limited', only 7 minutes late, and seen here emerging from Whiteball tunnel behind 4-6-0 No 6010 *King Charles I*. In contrast with the down trains, which had difficulty maintaining their scheduled headway, the up trains, with the advantage of easier gradients, were able to maintain headways of 5 minutes between trains, so that as there were slightly fewer up trains scheduled that day than on the down line, there were periodic gaps in the flow. These were useful to the signalman at Whiteball Siding, who could use them to return the banking engines to Wellington.

By mid-afternoon there was further evidence of the difficulties being experienced at Paignton, as the afternoon departures failed to materialise on time. The worst affected was the 1.55 pm from Torquay to Paddington, ten coaches behind 4-6-0 No 1011 *County of Chester*, which was 72 minutes late, contrasting with the preceding train, the 10.45 am from Penzance to Sheffield, 12 coaches behind 4-6-0 No 6996 *Blackwell Hall*, which had been 2 minutes early.

The 70 trains seen that afternoon - 34 up and 36 down - had been hauled by locomotives from only seven different classes: 7 'Kings', 21 'Castles', 4 'Counties', 27 'Halls' and 9 'Granges' (all 4-6-0s), 1 '51xx' 2-6-2T and 1 '63xx' 2-6-0. For the record, one train was double-headed and one I failed to record. But the figures demonstrate the degree of standardisation achieved by the GWR and its successor the Western Region.

18 June 1988

Auto-trailer memories

A whiff of genuine GWR nostalgia for branch-line lovers, this view was taken from the inside of ex-GWR auto-trailer No 168, while it was standing momentarily at Golant, mid-way along the line from Lostwithiel to Fowey on 29 July 1958. The comfortably upholstered but sturdy wooden seats are occupied by a mixture of eager tourists and locals on shopping trips.

As with most of the auto-trailers built for branch-line use, the seating is arranged transversely in the centre of the saloon, but with long bench-style seats adjacent to the picture windows at either end. Alongside these bench seats, which give plenty of room for standing passengers, are arranged a row of stout leather straps suspended from ceiling brackets, from which passengers tall enough to be able to reach them can support themselves.

Down the centre line of the white-painted ceiling, the electric light bulbs are arranged in groups of three, each group within a large circular moulding. In earlier times this moulding would have supported a large inverted glass dome enclosing the gas mantles, with which earlier trailers had been equipped. However, this batch, built at Swindon in 1929, were the first trailers to be given electric lighting when new, and an earlier design was evidently adapted - possibly the electric lighting was a last-minute decision.

Also protruding from the ceiling on either side are the typical GWR design of ventilator, while immediately below them, running along the top of the windows, is the conduit carrying the communication cord - penalty for misuse 40 shillings, I believe, at that time.

Above the main windows are inward-opening hammered glass ventilators, and set into the edge of the window frames - visible above the arm of the gentleman who is regarding my activities with great interest - are the notches to accept the pins on either end of the lower edge of the roller blind, which could be pulled down to keep the sun out. The staff were instructed to pull down these blinds if the coach was to be out of use for any length of time, so that the sun would not fade the upholstery.

At the far end of the saloon can be seen the row of photographs, without which no GWR passenger compartment was complete. The pictures were always of places somewhere on the GWR: rural scenes, street scenes, beaches, places of interest, events such as point-to-point races, and of course the GWR's own hotels at Paddington, Fishguard, the Manor House near Moretonhampstead, and the Tregenna Castle at St Ives.

In these auto-trailer saloons even the panel between the windows contained long vertical strip pictures, suitable for GWR favourites such as Symonds Yat, Cheddar Gorge or Thatcher Pines on the edge of Torbay.

Sadly, although the Lostwithiel to Fowey line is still in daily use over most of its length for clay export traffic, it lost its passenger service in 1965, and a journey along the densely wooded banks of the river, with the sun sparkling on the water as 0-4-2 tank No 1419 made light work of its single auto-trailer, can now only be made in the memory.

25 June 1988

Change at Heathfield

One station much frequented by auto-trailers of the type seen in the previous picture was Heathfield, at the junction of the Moretonhampstead and Teign Valley lines.

Pictured on 7 June 1958, the last day on which passenger trains operated over the Teign Valley line, we are looking towards Moretonhampstead, as the 4.35 pm from Exeter St David's, headed by 2-6-2T No 5536, runs into the bay platform provided for Teign Valley trains. In the up platform 0-4-2 tank No 1427 stands ready to propel the auto-trailers forming the 5.10 pm from Moretonhampstead on to Newton Abbot, after any passengers from the Teign Valley train have made the cross-platform connection.

When originally opened in 1874, Chudleigh Road station, as Heathfield was then named, had only the one platform - at which No 1427 now stands - on the broad gauge single line to Moretonhampstead.

The completion of the standard gauge Teign Valley Railway from Ashton into Chudleigh Road station in 1882 - the line on which No 5536 is approaching - brought about the change of name to Heathfield, as the Teign Valley Railway had its own Chudleigh station situated on the outskirts of the village.

For the next ten years, until the broad gauge was abandoned in May 1892, the broad gauge Moretonhampstead line and the standard gauge Teign Valley Railway existed side by side, but with no physical connection between the two, save for adjacent sidings on which goods could be laboriously transhipped from wagon to wagon.

Even after 1892 only an indirect connection was at first provided between the two lines. It was not until 1916 that a direct connection, which did not involve reversal, was installed, at which time the signal box was relocated and the platform extended.

Appropriately, the new signal box was built using buff-coloured bricks from the adjacent Great Western Pottery and Brick and Tile Works, owned by Candy Tiles Ltd, whose immense chimneys dominated the local landscape for many years. This factory had had its own private siding since 1887.

The next major change to Heathfield station came in 1927, when a crossing loop was provided for Moretonhampstead line trains and a new down platform was constructed adjacent to the Brick and Tile Works.

The final stage in the station's development came in 1943, when a double junction was provided connecting both up and down Moretonhampstead lines to the Teign Valley line, in conjunction with an extension of the crossing loop in the Newton Abbot direction.

At the same time crossing loops were also extended at Trusham and Christow and a new one was installed at Longdown. This was in anticipation of greatly increased traffic, in the form of Ambulance Trains to the US Army hospital at Stover, in the months following D-Day in 1944, which fortunately turned out not to be as great as had been feared.

This layout then remained in use until well after both lines had closed to passengers, though it has been pointed out to me recently that a small change made by the late summer of 1958 was the addition of fixed distant arms below both starting signals for the Teign Valley line. This was probably an indication to crews of the freight trains which continued to use this line that the services of the lady crossing keeper at Bovey Lane had been dispensed with and it would now be necessary for them to stop and open the crossing gates themselves.

2 July 1988

Luxulyan

Luxulyan was in 1958 one of several crossing stations on the mainly single-track Cornish branch line from Par to Newquay; although it is, perhaps, unfair to class this as a true branch line, because on Fridays and Saturdays during the period of the summer timetable it carried many full-length trains destined for London and various up-country industrial cities.

In some ways it resembled the Kingswear branch, which was able to accept the heaviest GWR locomotives and trains, except that in the case of the Cornish line the heaviest passenger locomotives it was required to carry were the 'Castle' Class 4-6-0s, because the 'King' Class 4-6-0s were not permitted to cross into Cornwall over the Royal Albert Bridge at Saltash.

Situated on the fringe of the main Cornish clay-mining area, almost in the shadow of the vast conical spoil tips which in those days gave this district its distinct 'Cornish clay' signature, Luxulyan is a village of stone dwellings built with material from the many once active local quarries. In those days Luxulyan had its own rail-served Treskilling clay works, the roof and chimney of which can be seen on the right of the picture.

Partially hidden by the foreground terrace of stone cottages is the unusual single-storey station building, situated well back from the island platform, on which is a typical GWR 'pagoda'-style corrugated iron waiting shelter.

As befits this picturesque location, a clerestory 'Camp Coach' stands at the buffer stop of the siding next to the station building, the 1930s wheeled version of today's holiday flat or cottage.

Before the island platform was constructed in 1910, to enable longer trains to be accommodated, the station had two very short platforms, placed on either side of the running tracks, finishing short of the water tower standing to the left of the Newquay-bound track.

This water tower was itself the subject of an unusual experiment in windpower, which was illustrated in the June 1906 edition of the *Great Western Railway Magazine*. The stone tower on which the water tank is mounted was then not so tall as it later became - the extra height, as can be seen, was added in a darker stone - and the magazine illustration shows a saddle tank engine taking water beside an enormous steel tower, quite three times the height of the water tank. On top of the steel tower is mounted a circular windmill with a fan tail, very reminiscent of those employed in the USA around that time.

The windmill was operating a water pump used to refill the tank, which presumably would otherwise have had to be done by hand. The magazine notes that the trial had been conducted under favourable conditions, though to avoid damage to the machine it had had to be stopped on one or two occasions, 'in consequence of an inconvenient surplus of the element necessary for driving it', they said. How long the experiment lasted is not known.

In 1958, peak summer Saturdays saw a mixture of 38 long-distance and local non-corridor trains on the branch, and this train is the 11.15 am from Newquay to Wolverhampton, hauled by 4-6-0s Nos 6941 *Fillongley Hall* and 6931 *Aldborough Hall* on 19 July 1958. It is painful to record that this summer there are just 12 services on the line on Saturdays, all of them provided by High Speed Train sets.

9 July 1988

A drink at St David's

Water, or rather the possible lack of it, has always been the 'Achilles' heel' of the steam engine, and elaborate precautions were taken in steam days to ensure that an adequate supply was always available, wherever it might be needed. Because steam was the driving force, it followed that the more work the engine had to do, the more water it would use. Consequently, on a long-distance run with a heavy train, although starting with a full tender holding 4,000 gallons, this would only be enough for part of the journey, and the tender tank would need to be topped up several times during a non-stop run from Plymouth to London. For this purpose, on suitably level sections of track at intervals of around 50 miles, troughs kept full of water were laid between the rails, from which the water could be transferred to the tender of a passing engine by means of a scoop beneath the tender, operated by the fireman of the engine.

In this way, several thousand gallons of water could be transferred from trough to tender in a few seconds. However, to do this the train had to be travelling at a reasonable speed and the trough had to be full, conditions which did not always apply on the busy peak summer Saturdays of the late 1950s.

Our picture shows the situation which could arise when these conditions were not met and a train which should have passed through Exeter St David's station non-stop, with a clear road ahead, has instead had to stop for water.

Clearly, for some reason the fireman did not collect enough water from the troughs at Powderham to enable him to get safely through to the next set of troughs at Creech St Michael, on the far side of Taunton, and an unscheduled 4-minute stop is being made to refill the tender, risking further delay to following trains. Both driver and fireman are on the platform; the fireman, in coal-black overalls and beret, has

inserted the bag of the water crane (out of sight beyond the top of the picture) into the tender, and now holds the chain with which he can swing it back across the platform after the driver, only the hand and shadow of whom can be seen, has turned off the water supply, both being careful to avoid the splash of water across the platform as the crane swings back into place.

Meanwhile, on this busy Saturday 3 August 1957, 'Castle' Class 4-6-0 No 5052 *Earl of Radnor* rolls into platform No 1 with train number 147, the 12.05 pm from Paddington to Plymouth, passing ex-Southern Railway 0-6-2T No 32697, which is waiting to provide banking assistance up to Central station for the next Southern train to arrive at platform No 3.

Here on platform No 5, 4-6-0 No 6025 *King Henry III* waits impatiently, raucously blowing off steam under the signal gantry, eager to get the 12.30 pm from Newquay to Paddington on its non-stop way again.

A scattering of coal lies on the platform where successive firemen have swept off their cab floors after damping down the coal with the 'pet' pipe, which now hangs idly down across No 6025's number plate.

A single gas lamp waits for evening to cast its mellow glow on the platform, perhaps to comfort the plain white china teacup seeking shelter by nestling at the foot of the water column. But it is still some months before winter frosts will add the occasional glow of fire from the 'devil', the curious metal box with double-headed chimney used to keep the crane arm from freezing up.

30 July 1988

Country holidays (1)

Whilst researching for an earlier 'Rail Trail' article about traffic on the Great Western Railway in the mid-1930s, I was somewhat mystified by frequent references in the Weekly Amendments to the Working Timetable to 'CCHF parties', some of which were sufficiently large to need special trains.

A kind friend solved the mystery by lending me a copy of a GWR 'Notice of Special Arrangements in connection with the Children's Country Holiday Fund parties from and to Paddington', leaving on Thursday 10th and returning on Thursday 24 August 1939.

The Children's Country Holiday Fund is a charity devoted to providing holidays in the country for children from poor families, many of whom in those days, even if they were working, would not have been able to afford a holiday away from home. Indeed, before the war many workers did not get any holidays with pay, apart from the statutory Bank Holidays.

That these children were expected to be a pretty unruly lot seems to be indicated by the instructions to the guards of the trains on which they were to travel: 'Guards working these trains to see that the doors on the off side are locked when the trains come to platform, and that the doors on the platform side are locked before departure of the train'. They were to be securely locked in for the whole of their journey, and also they were to be cautioned by the Station Master himself not to interfere with the communication cord.

That this caution seemed likely to be ineffective, on what may for many of these children have been their first long journey by train, is shown when the notice continues: 'In the event of a train being stopped by this means, the guard must obtain the full name and address of the offender'. Some hopes!

The children were going to country stations all over the GWR system. The list would have been familiar to Dr Beeching in 1963, when he was writing his report and proposing the closure of many of them. Through Oxfordshire, Worcestershire and Herefordshire, into Wales and the South West, they were distributed deep into the heartland of the GWR, over 4,000 children travelling on 18 different trains out of Paddington, including three Specials. Some went no further than the Thames valley, to Maidenhead, Pangbourne and Tilehurst, while others went on to Stow-on-the-Wold, Stratford-upon-Avon and Henley-in-Arden.

Some children had several changes of train, such as those heading for Dingestow and Raglan Road Crossing Halt on the little-used line from Monmouth (Troy) to Pontypool Road, who had to change at Ross-on-Wye and Monmouth (Troy).

The numbers to be accommodated at the various places fluctuated wildly, from groups of two children going to Williton, on the Minehead line, or three to Ashton, in the Teign Valley, to groups of 198 to Pensford and 288 to Bromyard. Twenty children arrived at Torre station at 1.28 pm, having travelled down on the 9.00 am from Paddington.

Our picture is of a typical train on which they might have travelled home along the seawall at Teignmouth, 14 coaches behind 'Star' Class 4-6-0 No 4021, originally named *King Edward* but re-named *British Monarch* in 1927.

6 August 1988

Country holidays (2)

The week after the previous article on the Children's Country Holiday Fund appeared, I was delighted to receive a letter from a reader of the newspaper who had first-hand knowledge of the pre-war CCHF.

Mrs Rachel Stephenson, who was a newly married teacher in Herefordshire in the summer of 1939, but who now lives in Preston, Paignton, remembers her journey vividly - but let her tell you the story in her own words.

'Last week's research into traffic on the GWR with reference to the CCHF . . . attracted my attention - I read on - Thursday 24 August 1939 - parties of children from poor families were returning to London after two weeks holiday in the country.

'Surely, I thought, surely that was the day that I had escorted a party of such children back to Paddington at the end of their two happy weeks in the heart of Herefordshire. I read on - parties of children went to all parts of the country from the Thames valley to Devon. Places such as Ross-on-Wye, Monmouth, Stow-on-the-Wold - all familiar to me - then surprise, oh, surprise, *Bromyard* had taken in 288 children - sleepy little Bromyard in the heart of rolling agricultural land in Herefordshire. Bromyard, where my late husband and two daughters were born, its Queen Elizabeth Grammar School where I was educated, its 800-year-old Parish Church of St Peter, where I was married in 1939.

'The children had all been placed with local people, from cottagers to hop- or dairy-farmers in the area. Activities, with which I was involved, were organised in the various Church Halls, and I believe it was our vicar of St Peter's who asked me if I would travel with this party of excited children back to Paddington.

'This finally achieved, I remember having a few hours on my own in Regent Street. It was then I realised how near we were to war being declared. People were feverishly buying up black-out material for curtains - something we hadn't even thought about in sleepy Bromyard.'

The train on which Mrs Stephenson and her CCHF charges travelled had started from Lyonshall at 8.40 am - the lamps there were extinguished for the last time very shortly afterwards, in July 1940 - and calling at Pembridge, Leominster, Bromyard, Worcester (Shrub Hill), Pershore and Moreton-in-Marsh, arrived at Paddington at 1.55 pm.

Her memory of the city population preparing for the black-out recalls that it was exactly one week later the order was given for the evacuation of all children from the capital. These same children would then have been a tiny part of the vast number undertaking a more permanent and less happy journey into the country. In a tremendous feat of organisation the GWR carried over 44,000 children and their teachers on the first day, using 50 trains of 12 coaches each, some trains making more than one journey.

The operation was centred on Ealing Broadway station, with the children arriving via the Underground to embark on GWR trains which departed at 9-minute intervals, monopolising the down relief line. Altogether almost 113,000 evacuees were carried on these special trains in four days, while a restricted normal service was also maintained.

Many of the special trains would have been hauled by GWR 'Moguls', although No 4322, seen in this picture leaving Dawlish with a down Exeter to Paignton stopper several years earlier, had been withdrawn from service in 1937.

20 August 1988

'Par, change for Newquay'

Thus the station nameboard both informs and instructs, in that succinct way so beloved of the railway sign constructors. In those days railway signs were made to last and were usually either cast iron plates with the words embossed, or large wooden boards with individually attached lettering, in this case the latter.

Attached to the side of the footbridge from which this photograph is taken, so that it is visible to passengers alighting on to the platform below, is another sign equally short and to the point, 'NEWQUAY TRAINS OVER THE BRIDGE', directing passengers to the far side of the island platform from which all Newquay trains depart before taking the sharp curve to the right, round to St Blazey then on up the grinding curves of the scenically wooded Luxulyan valley.

We are looking down the main line towards St Austell and Truro on Saturday 2 July 1960 as the 11.10 am (Saturdays only) from Penzance to Birmingham and Wolverhampton draws into the station. On weekdays this is 'The Cornishman' express, but on Saturdays in the summer it is denied this dignity, although 13 coaches long and hauled by two engines.

The pilot engine in front is 4-6-0 No 7820 *Dinmore Manor*, the first of the 1950 batch of 'Manors' built by British Railways at Swindon to the GWR design, while the train engine is 4-6-0 No 6837 *Forthampton Grange*, built by the GWR at Swindon in 1937. Incidentally, the basic structure of No 7820, after many years in the Barry scrapyard, is now being restored, for eventual service on the West Somerset Railway.

However, to return to Par station, this today is one of the very few left in the West Country where the signalman in his box still watches over the station and pulls the levers to operate the points and signals in the traditional manner, but many of the other details in our picture have changed.

The large water tank standing aloft behind the signal box has gone, and with it the water columns at each end of the station platforms, from which the steam engines could replenish their tanks and tenders. Likewise the telegraph poles and wires have been replaced by underground cables.

The station is no longer gas-lit as it was in 1960, with an elegant row of graceful chocolate-and-cream-painted columns down each platform.

Before the days of the now all-conquering black plastic bin-liner, rubbish was disposed of into a wire mesh basket, one of which stands alongside the station nameboard, which also has a vintage shunter's pole leaning against it, another feature of the railway scene which is now rarely seen.

At the far end of the platform a pair of enginemen are seated upon one of the many ex-GWR four-wheeled steerable flat barrows, which has been thoughtfully left there for this purpose. Others are liberally scattered around the station; one on the up platform bears a rather lonely - not to say lost - looking mailbag and two china cups.

With the 6.50 am from Paddington to Penzance running on time and already signalled, the passengers on the down platform will soon be taken on their way to St Austell or Truro behind 4-6-0 No 6824 *Ashley Grange*, and 2 minutes later the unlikely combination of 4-6-0 No 7921 *Edstone Hall* and 0-6-0 pannier tank No 7709 will arrive from Newquay with a local train terminating at Par.

27 August 1988

Penzance

Another visit to Cornwall takes us to the end of the GWR main line at Penzance, with a view over the terminus taken on 14 July 1962.

The photograph shows the station area substantially as reconstructed and enlarged by the GWR in 1937, although the walls and roof of the station building date back to 1879. This building replaced the original West Cornwall Railway terminus, once described in the local press as 'a large dog's house of the nastiest and draughtiest kind', which had been opened in 1852, when the earlier Hayle Railway was developed into a through line from Truro to Penzance.

At the time of the West Cornwall Railway's opening in 1852, for reasons of economy built to the standard gauge, the Cornwall Railway was still constructing its broad gauge line from Plymouth to Truro, which did not open until 1859. Consequently, after the opening of the Cornwall Railway there was a break of gauge at Truro, which lasted until 1866 when an additional broad gauge rail was extended to Penzance.

At that time the Penzance terminus building was a very short low-roofed wooden structure, barely reaching the height of the wall supporting the road alongside, and accommodating only two mixed gauge tracks. On its seaward side was an inconveniently small goods yard, engine shed and goods shed, one side of which also formed part of the seawall, which then stood where the two ex-LMSR coaches are standing in the foreground of our picture.

Upon taking over the West Cornwall Railway in 1876, the GWR immediately drew up plans for enlargement of the goods facilities by building a new engine shed to the east of the station, and later, in 1878, for the rebuilding of the station itself. The present station building seen in the background of the picture was completed in 1879, though then with only two short platforms, sufficient for the broad gauge trains of that period, and a spare track down the centre for stock. When the broad gauge rails were removed after 1892, it was possible to lengthen the platforms a little and to add a further track under the roof.

Although in the period of the GWR's great expansion during the Edwardian era an attempt was made to further enlarge the station site, this was opposed by the Council, and further substantial development had to wait another 30 years. It was not until 1937 that the station site was eventually enlarged to the situation shown in our 1962 picture, by reclaiming a large area from the sea and rebuilding the seawall from Albert Pier, in the left background, for 1,000 feet eastwards towards Ponsandane.

Meanwhile, in 1914, the engine shed had again been moved from the rather cramped 1876 site just east of the station to a new and commodious location at Long Rock, opposite St Michael's Mount and not far short of the station at Marazion.

At long last Penzance had a station worthy of the 'Cornish Riviera Express' - it could hold four 12-coach trains, and had separate covered loading facilities for the considerable perishable traffic, both from local producers and from the Isles of Scilly. This traffic was handled under the roof which can be seen behind the 6-car diesel multiple unit train in platform No 4.

In the foreground is the 4.45 pm from Penzance to Manchester, shortly to set off hauled by 4-6-0 No 1001 *County of Bucks*, which should know the way quite well, having travelled this route many times in its younger days when allocated new to Newton Abbot in 1945.

17 September 1988

Plymouth North Road

When this picture was taken, on 23 March 1961, Plymouth's North Road station was in the final stages of a re-building programme which had commenced over 20 years earlier, before the outbreak of war in 1939.

Even prior to 1939, North Road station was in desperate need of improvement, its last major facelift having taken place way back in 1908; its short up- and down-side train sheds and wooden office buildings presented a poor impression to the intending traveller.

By the time work on the improvements was halted, at the outbreak of war, the up side of the new station had been more or less completed, with a new platform layout, modern refreshment and waiting rooms and individual awnings for each island platform. But on the down side the old train-shed remained in use until the mid-1950s, together with the old wooden office buildings.

It was not until the 1955 Modernisation Plan was announced that money again became available for major improvement works and the new plans included an office tower block in the style - or lack of it - fashionable at that time; it is the skeleton of this which can be seen rising above the down platforms in our picture. The down side had by then been reconstructed to the new layout and already all the old semaphore signals had been replaced by colour lights, controlled from a new signal box at the far (west) end of the station. At that time the new panel box only controlled the signals within the station area, but today it is responsible for operations between Liskeard and Totnes.

Although the South Devon Railway opened to Plymouth in 1849, North Road station did not come into existence until 1877. It was preceded in 1871 by Mutley station - situated about 100 yards east of the point from which this picture was taken - which closed in 1939 to allow the improvements to North Road to commence.

Before that the only Plymouth station was the terminus at Millbay, which continued to handle most of the local services and stopping trains on the main line until its premature closure in 1941, when destruction of the goods shed alongside by enemy bombing resulted in its passenger platforms being permanently converted for use as an alternative goods shed. It had only moderate-length platforms and had long since ceased to be used by the through trains to Cornwall, so its closure was only an inconvenience to those who either worked or lived in its vicinity.

In its heyday North Road was an extremely busy station, handling not only the GWR main-line trains but also the intensive local service between Plympton and Saltash, the Launceston and Yealmpton branch trains and the LSWR (later SR) trains originating from Plymouth Friary station on their way to Devonport and thence round the northern flank of Dartmoor to Exeter.

In this picture ex-GWR 4-6-0 No 1006 *County of Cornwall* is leaving on the up 'Cornishman' express from Penzance to Wolverhampton, while behind on the left is No D6332 with an up fitted van train, possibly traffic from Millbay Docks, and, on the right, 'Warship' Class No D840 *Resistance* waiting to leave on the 1.15 pm to Liverpool.

1 October 1988

Christmas Eve

The lights of Newton Abbot West box reflect off the side of ex-GWR 'Castle' Class 4-6-0 No 4037 *The South Wales Borderers* as she stands beneath the old GWR wooden post bracket signal that controlled exit westwards from Newton Abbot's platforms Nos 2 and 4 in December 1961.

Out of sight above, the water crane has been swung across and No 4037's tender is being filled with two or three thousand gallons of water. Ahead, steam leaks from the cylinder cocks and the safety valves are just on the sizzle.

By late 1960 most of the regular express trains were already diesel-hydraulic hauled, but Christmas Eve 1960 saw a welcome influx of steam engines on the many relief trains provided for the holiday weekend. My own travels that day went no further than Exeter, on the 3.09 pm from Torre, travelling in what was then an almost brand new diesel railcar, passing at Teignmouth and Dawlish both parts of the 9.00 am from Wolverhampton. Unusually, both were double-headed, the first by 4-6-0s Nos 6905 *Claughton Hall* and 4904 *Binnegar Hall*, the second by 4-6-0s Nos 6995 *Benthall Hall* and 7030 *Cranbrook Castle*. At the Warren, 4-6-0 No 4079 *Pendennis Castle* passed on the first part of the 'Torbay Express', while behind it, at Starcross, was No D804 *Avenger* on the 'Torbay Express' proper.

Approaching Exeter St Thomas we passed 4-6-0 No 6965 *Thirlestaine Hall* pulling out with the relief to the down Swansea, while the main train behind No D818 *Glory* was just leaving St David's as we ran in.

Exeter St David's station, having recently dispatched six trains to the West, was having a breather, although, as usually, there was plenty going on. Ex-Southern Railway 'N' Class 2-6-0 No 31836 came rushing down the bank from Central with the 4.21 pm from Exeter Central to Torrington, as 4-6-2

No 34032 *Camelford* drifted into platform No 3 with a portion of the 4.30 pm from Central to Waterloo.

After an exchange of hoots and whistles between *Camelford* and the 'Z' Class 0-8-0T banker, the 'Pacific' shuffled off up the bank chased by the raucous tank at the rear of the train.

Meanwhile, last-minute shoppers and early homeward-bound workers, escaping from the office party, were boarding the crowded Exe Valley auto-trailers in the bay platform, which left behind 0-6-0T No 9765, to be replaced soon after by 2-6-2T No 5508 which arrived with an inward Exe Valley train.

Ex-Southern Railway 'M7' Class 0-4-4T No 30125 paused, before climbing up to Central on a short freight train, while ex-GWR 2-8-0 No 3856 took advantage of the gap in the down passenger trains to leave via the freight lines and out past West box and over the river with a long loose-coupled goods train.

Station shunting was being performed by 0-6-0T No 5412 at the west end and by 0-4-2T No 1471 up by the Red Cow crossing.

In due course 4-6-0 No 1021 *County of Montgomery* clattered in over the crossing with the Paignton-bound first part of the 1.30 pm from Paddington, to be followed by 4-6-0 No 6959 *Peatling Hall* on the late-running relief to the down Liverpool, on which I travelled back to Newton Abbot.

Which brings us full circle, as the next train in was the 9.05 am from Liverpool, conveying through carriages to Plymouth and Kingswear, which is the train shown in the picture, although on Christmas Eve 1960 it had arrived behind 4-6-0 No 5024 *Carew Castle*, which had been replaced at Newton by 4-6-0 No 6983 *Otterington Hall*. My journey home to Torre was safely accomplished behind 2-6-2T No 4561.

24 December 1988

PASSENGERS MUST
NOT CROSS THE LINE
EXCEPT BY MEANS
OF THE FOOTBRIDGE

Mary Tavy & Blackdown

The South Devon & Tavistock Railway's Bill received the Royal Assent in 1854, but it was to be June 1859 before the citizens of Tavistock could celebrate the arrival of the first train in their town.

With Tavistock now firmly established on the railway map, Launceston - which had been in decline for some years - now had to decide whether to continue to hope for the arrival of a direct 'narrow' (standard) gauge line from Exeter, or to try for an extension of the Tavistock line.

In making this decision the town was assisted by the South Devon Railway, which was always fearful of the narrow gauge LSWR eventually invading 'its' territory - and in 1862 the Launceston & South Devon Railway Bill was proposed for 19 miles of railway from Launceston via Lifton, Coryton, Lidford, (later Lydford) and Mary Tavy to join the existing line at Tavistock.

The Bill was passed with only minor amendments and a contract for the work was signed in April 1863. Two years later the line was ready for opening, and on 1 June 1865 two South Devon Railway engines, *Dart* and *Giraffe*, hauled the 14-coach opening train out from Plymouth. This turned out to be a little premature, as the Inspecting Officer of Railways was not entirely satisfied that all the fences were complete, and consequently opening to the public was delayed until 1 July 1865.

Traffic on the new section was well up to expectations, and although the number of passengers fluctuated, the goods traffic rose steadily. Launceston had previously had to rely on the 4-mile-distant Bude Canal for transport of heavy goods into the town, and the arrival of the railway reduced the price of coal by 25 per cent. The town now prospered and the railway company even declared a small dividend. Nevertheless, there were still those who hankered after the direct connection to Exeter, and the South Devon Railway did not help matters by providing inconveniently timed trains and then reducing the initial service of five daily trains to three in 1872.

However, by 1875, with the narrow gauge tracks of the LSWR now open from Exeter via Okehampton as far as Lidford, the five-train service was restored and the branch from Lidford to Marsh Mills was about to enter its busiest period.

A clause had been inserted into the Tavistock Railway's Bill requiring it to lay a third narrow gauge rail, if such a line should eventually connect itself from the north and desire access to Plymouth. That day had now arrived. Needless to say, the South Devon Railway - which by now had absorbed both the Tavistock and Launceston companies - did not rush to comply and took two years to complete the job.

It was thus not until May 1876 that LSWR trains first entered Plymouth using the single track branch line from Lidford to Marsh Mills, thence via the South Devon Railway's main line to Mutley and on to the LSWR's new terminus at Devonport.

This picture shows Mary Tavy & Blackdown on 23 September 1961. By then an unstaffed halt for 20 years, Mary Tavy had been a very busy crossing station during the years 1876 to 1890, when this single line also carried the LSWR trains on their way to Devonport.

In view of the almost indecent haste with which redundant buildings are often swept away today, it is interesting to note that although the crossing loop, down platform and signal box were all taken out of use in 1892, both the signal box and down waiting shelter were still in existence in 1961.

31 December 1988

'County' at Truro

Ex-GWR 'County' Class 4-6-0 No 1001 *County of Bucks* starts the 3.40 pm Penzance to Paddington train - carrying perishable traffic to the London markets - from Truro on 9 September 1961. Inside the engine's cab the driver has turned to wave to a colleague, revealing the handle of the reversing lever, which is in full forward gear for the departure. Once the train is well on the move, the driver will gradually wind the gear back nearer to the mid-position, until at full speed the Stephenson valve gear - located between the frames - will be admitting steam alternately to either end of the cylinders for only about 25 per cent of the piston stroke.

This will be enough to keep the train going at speed, with a fairly full regulator opening, until an adverse gradient is reached, when the gear will be wound forward to give an increase in the admission of steam to the cylinders and consequently more power.

Above the handle of the reversing lever can be seen the white dial of the speedometer, a feature which was not fitted to this class until the early 1950s.

Since the GWR had been fitting speedometers to its express engines since the mid-1930s, this omission was probably due to shortage of the equipment in the immediate post-war years, as certain 'Castle' Class engines built new in 1946 also appeared without speedometers.

When the first 4-6-0 'County', No 1000 *County of Middlesex*, appeared in August 1945, it was equipped with a reasonably handsome copper-capped double chimney, and also heralded the return of peacetime conditions with full lining out, after the plain green of the express engines during the war. But subsequent members of the class all appeared with single chimneys, though still with the new record high boiler pressure of 280 lbs per sq in.

By the time this picture was taken the whole class had had their boiler pressure reduced to 250 lbs per sq in, and had been re-draughted with squat double chimneys, which sat uneasily on the 5-foot diameter smokebox.

The straight nameplates were also an unusual feature of the 'Counties', brought about by the fitting of one continuous splasher over the 6 ft 3 in diameter driving wheels. On the other side of the engine the nameplate could be attached direct to the top of the splasher, but on this side the reversing lever got in the way and the nameplate had to be mounted separately.

The post-war 'Counties' were never quite as successful as had been hoped and probably did their best work in Devon and Cornwall, and on the undulating GWR main line between Wolverhampton and Chester.

No 1001 *County of Bucks* came brand new to Newton Abbot in September 1945 and for some time was employed on the daily stopping service between Newton Abbot and Penzance, a journey on which the full effect of the explosive exhaust produced by a combination of high boiler pressure and expert Swindon valve setting, could be enjoyed to the full.

Alongside the steps leading up to the signal box is the duty signalman's bicycle, a reminder that even in the early 1960s few railwaymen could afford cars, and most either walked, cycled or bussed to work.

In the centre of the picture stands a fine example of a GWR wooden post starting signal, with the arm lowered into the 'off' position, while to the left is a much less common GWR backing signal. When lowered this indicated only that the road was correctly set for the line ahead, but not that the line was clear. This was useful for shunting out on to the main line under the control of a shunter.

14 January 1989

Heathfield connections

The scene is Heathfield, on the Moretonhampstead branch, at 10.45 am on 7 July 1956, following the arrival of 0-4-2T No 1427 on the 10.30 am from Newton Abbot, in the down platform, on the left-hand side of the picture. Normally this train would be the daily through working from Paignton, but as this is a summer Saturday it has only come from Newton Abbot, in order to keep the Kingswear branch line clear for main-line trains.

Due at Heathfield at 10.38 am, the train is 7 minutes late, and this accounts for the driver and fireman of 2-6-2T No 82001 on the 10.15 am from Moretonhampstead having taken up residence on the station seat alongside the engine.

As this latter train ran in there were at least 25 people on the platform to board it, and they are now waiting, probably impatiently, to commence their journey into Newton Abbot. But first the necessary single-line rituals must be performed, which will ensure that although the train from Moretonhampstead was first in, it will also be last out.

This situation arises because, being a single-line branch, each driver has to carry a token entitling him to be in the section shown on his token. As each token has to be returned to one of the machines in the signal boxes at either end of the section before another can be extracted, this ensures that only one train can be in any section at a time.

The fireman of No 82001 will have handed the token for the Bovey to Heathfield section to the signalman, who will have been waiting by his box at the far end of the platform to receive it. This token could then be returned to the machine and another one extracted ready to hand to the driver of No 1427 on the Newton Abbot to Moretonhampstead train as soon as it arrives.

The Newton Abbot to Heathfield token surrendered by No 1427 then has to be processed similarly, and it looks as though the signalman has just emerged from his box to commence the long walk down the platform to pass it to the driver of No 82001, who only then will be able to proceed to Newton Abbot.

No 82001 was the second of a class of 45 British Railways Standard Class '3' 2-6-2Ts. She was built at Swindon in April 1952 for branch-line duties and, together with most of the other BR Standard locomotives, had a comparatively short life, being withdrawn in January 1966 and subsequently scrapped by Cashmores at Newport. Despite being a Swindon product, the class were never popular locally - the cabs were reckoned to be hot in summer and draughty in winter, and although there were several at Newton Abbot in 1956 - Nos 82002/5 and 82034 were seen that same morning - they were later replaced by ex-GWR '51xx' tanks on these duties.

Waiting patiently in the background, at the bay platform, is ex-GWR 0-6-0T No 5412 on the Teign Valley train. This consists of a single ex-GWR auto-coach, one of many converted from steam railmotors during the 1930s. This is one of the branch-line series, having a centre entrance for the passengers and a guard's compartment at the far end.

Any passengers from the Newton Abbot train wishing to either leave the station or join the Teign Valley train will first have to walk across the track ahead of the engine, over the boarded crossing, as no footbridge was provided at Heathfield when the down platform was constructed in 1927. Not that one was really needed, with all trains stopping at this rural junction station, so typical of the many others around the country soon to be swept away in the march of - progress?

25 February 1989

Diversions

We are again at Exeter St David's station on a summer Saturday afternoon, but time has moved on and the diesel-hydraulic locomotives have now taken over most of the regular Western Region passenger trains.

However, steam engines still predominate on the Southern Region west of Salisbury, and also haul many of the summer extras, parcels and freight trains on the Western. But what, I hear the knowledgeable reader asking, is No D818 *Glory* doing descending from Exeter Central on train 1C28, which is the 9.30 am from Paddington to Newquay, on Saturday 26 August 1961?

The answer to this question lay on the other side of Westbury, where, five days earlier, at the London end of the 'cut-off' between Patney & Chirton and Westbury, a landslip had occurred which had effectively closed the main line. Consequently, on this summer Saturday all the numerous trains between Paddington and the West Country had to be found alternative routes.

Although those trains booked to call at Taunton and/or Westbury could be taken over the original single-line route through Devizes and Holt Junction, this had a very limited capacity and meant up to an hour's delay. Constraints also applied to the other alternative routes, and although diversion via Bristol might these days seem to be the obvious alternative, in 1961 Bristol already had more trains than it could cope with on an August Saturday. This option was used on later Saturdays in September, until the landslip had been repaired, but on this first Saturday more drastic emergency diversions were employed.

These involved four Western Region trains booked for non-stop running between Paddington and Plymouth (three up and one down), plus the 8.25 am from Paddington to Perranporth and Penzance, which had a booked call at Brent, for whose passengers alternative arrangements must have been made.

This would have been necessary because each of these trains made their way between Paddington and Plymouth via Reading, Basingstoke and thence over the Southern route through Salisbury, Exeter Central and St David's, Okehampton, Tavistock North, under the Royal Albert Bridge and into (or out of) Plymouth, where reversal was necessary.

At Exeter St David's one therefore had the unusual sight of trains between Paddington and Plymouth passing through the station in opposite directions, according to which route they had taken, and also trains travelling to and from Paddington overtaking each other on adjacent tracks.

This happened to the up 'Cornish Riviera Express' hauled by No D867 *Zenith*, which came up from Plymouth over the Southern route via Okehampton and hence arrived in Exeter St David's platform No 3 from the north. While it was standing there for 9 minutes attaching 'Z' Class 0-8-0Ts Nos 30956 and 30957 as bankers, it was overtaken in the same direction on the adjacent through line by the second part of the *down* 'Cornish Riviera Express' hauled by D827 *Kelly*. Rather more remarkable had been the appearance earlier in the afternoon of 4-6-0 No 6973 *Bricklehampton Hall*, which coasted down the bank from Exeter Central with the 8.25 am from Paddington to Perranporth and Penzance, having presumably worked the train through from Paddington, in which case this was almost certainly the only occasion on which a 'Modified Hall' worked throughout over this route.

The two trains not already mentioned which worked over the Southern route that afternoon were the 8.15 am Perranporth to Paddington behind D826 *Jupiter* and the 9.20 am St Ives to Paddington behind D852 *Tenacious*.

11 March 1989

Overnight parcels

At 9.20 am on a crisp February morning in 1952, Newton Abbot's only 'Britannia' Class 4-6-2 No 70022 *Tornado* climbs Dainton bank with the 6.25 am from Bristol to Plymouth. The 6.25 am Bristol was effectively a regular relief to the overnight 12.35 am from Manchester (London Rd) to Penzance, otherwise known as the 'North Mail', which trailed it, when on time, from Bristol at 6.45 am, to eventually stagger into Penzance at 2.30 pm, after stopping at 20 of the 21 stations then open on the main line through Cornwall - the sole exception was Probus & Ladock Platform.

One of the reasons for the extended journey time was the lengthy station stops that had to be endured at major junction stations - 34 minutes at Crewe, 40 at Bristol and 25 at Plymouth, with 8 to 10 minutes at each of the other main stations along the route.

As long as the Manchester train reached Bristol by 6.25 am - it was due in at 6.5 am - passengers for the main stations to Plymouth could at least change trains and go forward on the relief, but this was of no advantage to anyone travelling beyond Plymouth.

The long station stops were necessary in those days to enable the station staff to manhandle in and out of the train the vast quantity of parcels and miscellaneous traffic then being carried by these overnight trains, which were devoted more to the carriage of goods than they were to passengers.

The first van is either No 799 or 800, one of the red-painted Royal Mail sorting carriages that were allocated to this service. This carried mail to be sorted for West Country deliveries that had arrived at Bristol on the 7.10 pm from Newcastle.

The next vehicle is an ex-LMSR bogie parcels van travelling from Leeds to Penzance, which had arrived at Bristol on the 9.00 pm from Bradford. The remaining five vehicles are all ex-GWR in origin, the first being a full brake in place of the rostered van 3rd, followed by three 3rds - 3rd class passengers were not elevated to 2nd class until 1956 - and the last vehicle is a brake composite.

At Plymouth, after removing the Royal Mail van from this train, and six or more vans and coaches from the Manchester train, the two were combined to form the 11.15 am departure to Penzance, arriving there at 2.30 pm.

The return workings of these two sets of coaches are interesting, as they illustrate the somewhat leisurely progress often made by rolling-stock 40 years ago. The coaches from the 12.35 am Manchester returned thence remarkably quickly, leaving Penzance at 4.45 pm to arrive back at Manchester at 6.20 am next morning. But they then stood there all day until taking up their next working on the 12.35 am to Penzance. Consequently, they only managed a return trip between Manchester and Penzance every two days.

The set which arrived as the 6.25 am from Bristol made rather more humble progress back, as a series of stopping trains, commencing with the 6.10 pm from Penzance to Truro that evening. Next day it was the 7.30 am from Truro to Exeter, the 1.00 pm from Exeter to Taunton, and finally the 2.25 pm from Taunton to Bristol, arriving back there at 4.00 pm, where the coaches rested until 6.25 am next day. Consequently, this set of coaches only managed to complete a return trip between Bristol and Penzance every two days.

This explains why the carriage sidings of yesteryear were always full of coaches, when they should have been out earning their keep, as they are today.

18 March 1989

Ipplepen & Torbryan Joint

The story of the Ipplepen & Torbryan Joint Railway is similar to that of many now long-forgotten railways which flourished for a brief period in the middle of the 19th century, only to disappear into history as the industry which they existed to serve declined into obscurity.

As a result of the outbreak of the American Civil War in 1861, cotton supplies to the North of England mills were threatened, and some of the cotton barons cast about for an alternative source of income. One such, the somewhat unfortunately named Sir Walter de Slavery, foresaw that the West Indian sugar trade might also be affected and sought to benefit on both counts by developing what had until then been only a Devonian cottage industry.

In certain favoured locations, Devon farmers' wives had for centuries profited from a natural reaction within the Devonian red sandstone, when internal pressure combined with summer temperature brought about a flow of black treacle, which after straining through many layers of muslin could be refined into a delicious golden syrup. This, when combined with clotted cream on oven-fresh buns, was food for the gods.

Sir Walter had evidently heard about this modest enterprise during an earlier convalescence in Torquay and in 1861 hired a geologist, whom he then dispatched to South Devon. Within weeks they had located a rich vein of treacle-bearing rock in the Torbryan area and immediately negotiations were entered into for the construction of a railway to serve the proposed mine.

Local landowners were enthusiastic, so progress was swift. Although intended purely to serve the mine at Torbryan, in deference to the good citizens of Ipplepen, whose village the railway skirted, it was always known as the Ipplepen & Torbryan Joint.

Commencing from a junction with the South Devon Railway at the Totnes end of Dainton tunnel, the line turned westwards following the natural land contours to end 2 miles 22 chains away on the edge of Orleigh Common, from where an overhead bucket line was constructed to the valley below.

Our picture shows on the right the only portion of the line to remain in use, as a siding for the Totnes bankers, as 4-6-0 No 7921 *Edstone Hall* passes bankers Nos 5196 and 4174, on the 11.20 am Plymouth to Taunton on 29 July 1959.

Sir Walter's intention was to industrialise the extraction process, using one of his vacant mills in Lancashire to crush the ore and then refine the treacle. To work the line two diminutive second-hand Manning Wardle saddle tanks were acquired and converted to the broad gauge.

The two saddle tanks were named *Uncle Tom* (presumably after a certain Mr Cobleigh) and *Sir Walter*. They were housed overnight in the transfer sidings behind Dainton Sidings signal box, where a water tower was located, and any repairs needed were carried out in the South Devon Railway's Works at Newton Abbot.

Although the enterprise was moderately successful for a few years, it came to a premature end when, after the very hot summer of 1868, the London & North Western Railway suddenly gave notice that they would no longer carry this traffic during the summer months. Apparently the very hot weather had caused leakage of treacle from the ore wagons during the latter part of their journey, and although the LNWR always regarded itself as a rather superior railway, it had probably never been quite so stuck-up before!

Consequently, the last train over the line ran exactly 120 years ago today, and it could be said that the Ipplepen & Torbryan Joint Railway came to a sticky end on 1 April 1869.

1 April 1989

Dainton Sidings

To return to the real world, perhaps a few words about the true history of the sidings at Dainton summit might be interesting. In this picture we see ex-GWR 4-6-0 No 6814 *Enborne Grange* proceeding towards Totnes - after halting at the stop board seen on this side of the signal box - with a goods train bound for the yards at Tavistock Junction near Plymouth on 31 July 1959. Smoke still pours from the mouth of Dainton tunnel, and after the tail of this long train has cleared, the signalman will ring a bell at the far end of the tunnel to signal the banking engine, 2-6-2T No 4105, forward into the sidings on the right, where it will stop behind the signal box. Here it will have to wait until a path is available back to Aller Junction, as a train is already signalled on the up line towards Newton Abbot.

The cleared area on the right, beyond the trees, was once the site of one of Brunel's Italianate houses for the pumping engines which were intended to create the vacuum which would draw the Atmospheric trains up to the summit. The massive engines in this house, manufactured by Messrs Boulton and Watt of Soho, had already been installed, and the pipes laid, when the decision was made to abandon the enterprise and rely instead on locomotive haulage.

The first siding to be laid at Dainton summit was, therefore, probably on the south side (right-hand in this picture) to serve the pumping house. A similar long siding on the north side - almost hidden in this picture, and the one around which the previous story was constructed - was probably laid soon afterwards, when it became the practice to divide the early broad gauge goods trains into two portions at the foot of the bank, in this case at Totnes, before the days of permanent banking engines. The train engine would then take the front half of the train up to the summit, back it into the siding and then return to Totnes for the second half, coupling the two halves together again at the summit and continuing as one train to Newton Abbot.

The Dainton Sidings signal box seen in this picture was constructed in 1893, and by 1905 the three sidings on the south side had been installed to serve a large quarry. In the early years of this century this quarry was extensive enough to have its own locomotive, which took its water supply from a tank mounted on a stone tower, which was still there in the 1950s, though well overgrown by that time.

Until 1949 two sidings extended for some distance into the clearing where the Atmospheric pumping house had been, and a walk around the quarry at that time revealed vestiges of railway track several hundred yards away from the main line.

As tunnels go, Dainton tunnel is a minnow, being only 264 yards long, and the summit of the line is just inside this end. The tunnel is straight, so the view from the signal box of a train climbing from Newton Abbot is most unusual. Because of the steep gradient the engine's chimney comes into view first, followed by the smokebox and then the buffer beam - that is, of course, on those occasions when the tunnel is not full of smoke!

In the late 1950s the signalman had no mains services, heating was by coal fire, lighting by oil, and water was collected as required from a spring at the foot of the foreground embankment, adjacent to the down main line. This often dried up in the summer time, when water would be brought out from Newton Abbot by the banking engines.

8 April 1989

Royal Train (1)

Two immaculate 'Castle' Class engines approach the now demolished stone bridge which took the bridle path to Edginswell across the Kingswear branch tracks between Kingskerswell and Scott's bridge. Nowadays this location is more likely to be referred to as Kerswell Gardens, and the bridge which now spans the line is part of a metal one recovered from Dawlish Warren a few years ago.

The occasion, for such it was, was the Royal visit on 8 May 1956, part of a two-day Royal tour of the West Country which had started from Paddington at 7.30 pm on the previous evening.

The Royal Train is normally kept at the ex-LMSR Carriage Works at Wolverton between journeys and it had worked down to Kensington (Olympia) that morning, where stores had been loaded, before it proceeded to Old Oak Common to be stabled on No 18 shed road until it was due to leave for Paddington at 6.15 pm.

At Paddington, two main-line and three suburban trains had their platforms changed to enable platforms Nos 1 and 2 to be kept clear, No 1 for the Royal Train and No 2 for a screening train with all blinds drawn and doors locked.

The Royal Train, consisting of 11 vehicles weighing 493 tons and precisely 737 ft 8^1/$_2$ inches long (excluding the engines) was due to arrive from Old Oak Common at 6.35 pm.

The ex-Works engines which had been selected and specially prepared to haul the train on this occasion were 'Castle' Class 4-6-0s Nos 7024 *Powis Castle* and 5044 *Earl of Dunraven*. As can be seen from the picture, this preparation included scouring of the buffers, cylinder heads and inside valve covers, all of which were normally painted over, plus the rods and all the usual brass and copperwork.

The Royal Train was to leave for the West at 7.30 pm, passing Reading at 8.18 pm where it took the Berks & Hants line via Newbury, passed at 8.39 pm. A stop was made at Heywood Road Junction, just short of Westbury, to reverse the train formation on the triangle to Hawkeridge. If this had not been done the Queen's saloon would have been off the end of the platform at her eventual destination at Barnstaple, and she is not usually expected to jump down on to the ballast! The 'Castles' therefore detached at Heywood Road and the train was taken around to Hawkeridge by 4-6-0 No 4927 *Farnborough Hall*; there the 'Castles' were coupled up to the other end of the train and brought it into Westbury to top up the gas and water supplies.

At 10.33 pm it was on its way again, via Castle Cary to Athelney, where it diverted on to the now long-closed single line track to Durston via Lyng Halt, where it was due to stable for the night. The Castles retired to Taunton shed via Durston, and 4-6-0 No 4971 *Stanway Hall* was attached to the Athelney end of the train for the night.

Next morning ex-GWR 2-6-0s Nos 6372 and 6385 were booked to leave Taunton shed at 7.10 am to proceed to the overnight stabling point, from where the Royal Train was due to leave at 8.05 am for Barnstaple (Victoria Road). They must have presented a fine sight that morning - both engines were recently ex-Works and had been painted green and fully lined out for this special occasion, the first 'Moguls' to be so treated.

They later returned the empty Royal Train to Norton Fitzwarren, where the two 'Castles' were re-attached to bring the stock down to Goodrington, ready for the Royal departure to Cornwall at 11.00 pm that night from Torquay station.

15 April 1989

Royal Train (2)

Continuing the story of the Royal visit to the West Country in May 1956, while the Royal Train was being serviced in Goodrington sidings 4-6-0 No 6995 *Benthall Hall* was attached to the Paignton end of the train, and the two 'Castles' returned to Newton Abbot shed. An additional engine would be needed to work the train out of Torquay that evening and 4-6-0 No 4948 *Northwick Hall* was booked to leave Newton Abbot at 9.05 pm to join No 6995 at Goodrington.

The empty Royal Train was due to leave Goodrington for Torquay at 10.10 pm, headed by the two 'Hall' Class engines; at Torquay it was to be brought to a stand with the footplate of the leading engine opposite a white post with a white light, provided on the driver's side 77 yards in advance of the Torquay Up Starting Signal. This degree of precision ensured that the entrance to the Queen's saloon would be opposite the red carpet, and similar white posts were erected at every point at which the Royal Train was required to stop, even if only to change engines, as it would do at Aller Junction, where 4-6-0s Nos 7024 *Powis Castle* and 5044 *Earl of Dunraven* would again take over for the run into Cornwall.

Numerous speed restrictions ensured a comfortable journey down to Lostwithiel, where the Royal Train was due to arrive at the stabling point on the Fowey branch at 1.40 am. Here, 4-6-0 No 4906 *Bradfield Hall* was attached at the Lostwithiel end, while the 'Castles' made their way via Fowey to St Blazey shed for the night.

The following day, 9 May, after *Bradfield Hall* had drawn the Royal Train back into Lostwithiel, the two 'Castles', which had meanwhile come up the main line from St Blazey, were coupled up and then took the Royal Party westwards to Grampound Road, where they were due to leave the train at 10.00 am for a road journey into Truro.

Meanwhile, the empty Royal Train proceeded to Truro for servicing, being attended by 4-6-0 No 4099 *Kilgerran Castle*, while the train engines were being turned, ready for departure from Truro with the Royal Party at 12.50 pm. The Royal destination this time was Liskeard, where they were due at 2.15 pm after making a short stop on the main line at milepost 276, in the shadow of Restormel Castle.

During the next 3 hours, while the Royal Party were making their way by road to Launceston, the empty Royal Train had a much longer and more complicated journey to attain the same destination. The two 'Castles' first took the empty Royal Train into Plymouth North Road station where it was watered and 4-6-0 No 4908 *Broome Hall* was attached to the rear, to draw it down to Plymouth Millbay station, where the gas supplies were topped up.

At Millbay the empty train was handed over to the Southern Region, whose 'N' Class 2-6-0s Nos 31835 and 31844 had come around from their Friary depot to attach to the front of the train. This was now about to set off from Millbay in the direction of Cornwall, but diverging almost immediately on to Southern Region metals at Devonport Junction and proceeding via Bere Alston and Tavistock North to Meldon Junction, where a further reversal was made, this time on to the so-called 'Withered Arm', out through Halwill Junction to Launceston, where it was due to arrive at 5.23 pm, ready for the return journey back to London.

For this the Southern provided 'N' Class 2-6-0s Nos 31830 and 31845, pictured here on the long curved approach to Cowley Bridge Junction, outside Exeter, where after yet another reversal they handed the Royal Train back to the Western Region, and 4-6-0s *Powis Castle* and *Earl of Dunraven* resumed their interrupted journey back to Paddington.

22 April 1989

Bodmin (1)

The town of Bodmin is nearly 4 miles distant from the Cornish main line, and although a branch to it was promised when the original Cornwall Railway was being planned, this was one of several good intentions that went unfulfilled due to the usual dire shortage of capital when the line was eventually constructed, with completion in 1859.

Consequently, Bodmin had to wait a further 28 years for its connection to the main line, which did not arrive in the town until 1887, and was for the first five years an independent standard gauge line until the main line was converted from the broad gauge in 1892.

But during all this time Bodmin was not without a railway. For its size, from 1887, Bodmin must have been almost unique in this country, because it could boast of having two terminal stations, each within a few hundred yards of the town centre. While the new GWR terminus stood on high ground to the south of the centre, nestling in a valley close to the tightly packed stone dwellings on the northern edge of the town was the terminus of the much earlier Bodmin & Wadebridge Railway. This had been open since 1834 - 53 years before the GWR arrived - and was conceived, as were all Cornwall's earliest railways, purely as a local line to connect Bodmin to the sea at the port of Wadebridge. It was Cornwall's first railway to use steam locomotives - brought in by sea - and enabled the easy transport inland of sea-sand for manuring the fields, and also the export of stone from local quarries, as well as providing a rudimentary passenger service and cheaper access to the products of the Industrial Revolution, especially coal.

The Bodmin & Wadebridge Railway also became an aiming point in the London & South Western Railway's competitive drive westwards, after it had acquired it illegally in the late 1840s, when the LSWR itself had progressed no further westwards than Dorchester!

Just over 12 months after the GWR's arrival in Bodmin, a separate loop line was constructed out of the terminus and down to join the Bodmin & Wadebridge line at Boscarne Junction, thus giving direct access to Wadebridge from the GWR main line, after reversal in the GWR Bodmin station.

It was to be another seven years before the LSWR line from Waterloo was completed through to Wadebridge, and Padstow was not reached until 1899.

The GWR trains from Bodmin Road normally worked through only to Wadebridge, although some went on to Padstow with Southern Railway motive power, often an 'O2' Class 0-4-4 tank. The GWR used '45xx' Class 2-6-2 tanks almost exclusively in latter years, though it was not unknown for Southern engines to get through to Bodmin Road on occasions, and, as well as the 'O2s', Southern 'T9' Class 4-4-0s and 'N' Class 2-6-0s are known to have visited Bodmin Road.

This picture shows ex-GWR 2-6-2T No 4565 running into the Bodmin terminus with the 2.30 pm from Bodmin Road to Wadebridge on 27 May 1961, passing the fine GWR three-arm bracket signal protecting the station, under which a spare set of branch passenger coaches is stored.

30 December 1989

Bodmin (2)

We are still at Bodmin on 27 May 1961, standing on the same bridge, but now looking in towards the terminus, a low stone-built L-shaped building, mostly hidden from view by the typically Great Western water tower.

The line in from Bodmin Road is the one on the right, currently being used by ex-GWR 2-6-2T No 4552, while the sharply curved line on the left is the extension down to Boscarne Junction, providing the through connection on to Wadebridge and Padstow.

The approach to Bodmin's GWR station, re-named Bodmin General in BR days, is flanked by embankments covered with flowering rhododendrons, at their best at the end of May. On the right the flowers tumble in almost Mediterranean profusion right back to the goods yard, where the yard crane stands over one of the early railway containers, on its four-wheel flat truck.

Beyond this stands the goods shed, also built of local stone, with more vans within and beyond it. These are about to be pushed to the far end of the line, as No 4552 propels her train of loaded clay wagons back into the goods shed.

This is but the half-way stage of a complex operation to convey 16 loaded clay wagons from Boscarne Junction up to Bodmin and, after reversal, on to Bodmin Road. The first eight of these wagons - the ones seen in this picture - had been brought up from Boscarne Junction earlier in the day and left in the siding alongside the engine shed. At 1.50 pm 2-6-2T No 4552 arrived with the 1.23 pm passenger train from Wadebridge, and was replaced by 2-6-2T No 4565, which came off shed to take the train on to Bodmin Road at 1.55 pm.

Once the passenger was clear, No 4552 came back down the platform and picked up the loaded clays with their guard's van from the siding alongside the shed and pulled them into the station. She then backed them towards the bridge, in order to clear the points, and then ran around the train, stopping first to dive into the goods shed, where another guard's van was sorted out from a string of vans, and this, together with one of the vans, was placed on the run-round loop.

No 4552 was then attached to this end of the clays in the platform road, pulled them out under the bridge, pushed them back on the run-round loop to pick up the other guard's van, then pulled the whole lot out again and pushed them back into the goods shed, at which point this picture was taken.

No 4552 then detached the front guard's van from the rest of the train and retired to the shed for water, having cleared the platform and run-round loop for No 4565 which was about to arrive on the 2.30 pm Bodmin Road to Wadebridge (seen on the previous page).

Once the passenger train was clear, No 4552 emerged from the shed into the station, and as soon as the line was clear to Boscarne Junction she proceeded thence with the guard's van to pick up the other half of the train - split because of the steep gradient up to Bodmin.

She was back within 20 minutes with another eight clay wagons. This time it was a simple operation to run around the train, pull it out under the bridge, back it down on to the eight clays in the goods shed and, now with a guard's van at either end of the train, to leave with the 16 clays and a van on the mostly downhill run to Bodmin Road, arriving just in time to give the next passenger train, the 3.24 pm from Wadebridge, a clear road out of Bodmin.

This had been but 2 hours in the life of a quiet rural terminus, but wartime plans envisaged this line carrying much of the Cornish main-line traffic - as we will see overleaf.

6 January 1990

Bodmin (3)

Ex-GWR 2-6-2T No 5539 is spotlit by the evening sun as she runs into Bodmin General station on 18 March 1961 with the 3.24 pm from Wadebridge to Bodmin Road. The plume of steam still drifting in the still air shows that the driver has only seconds earlier closed the regulator, as his fireman leans out of the cab, single-line staff in hand, ready to pass this to the signalman, who will be standing on the platform ready to receive it. Alongside, 2-6-2T No 4565 is taking water from the overhead tank outside the single-road engine shed.

It is hard to imagine Bodmin as the scene of main-line operations, but during the 1939-45 war one of the recurring nightmares that must have afflicted the GWR's Superintendent of the Line, Gilbert Matthews, was the possibility that sooner or later the Royal Albert Bridge across the Tamar would become a target for German bombers.

In fact, the danger was probably less than would have been imagined at the time. Nevertheless, the possibility of the bridge being hit had to be faced, and detailed timetables were prepared for this eventuality, should it have occurred. The only alternative route into Cornwall was over the Southern Railway's North Cornwall line, from Exeter through Okehampton, forking right at Meldon Junction and then via Halwill Junction, Launceston and Delabole down to Wadebridge. Thence the route would run via the old Bodmin & Wadebridge line to Boscarne Junction, climbing up to Bodmin on the GWR branch line and down to Bodmin Road, where the GWR main line could be regained.

Not the least of the snags about this route was that from Meldon Junction to Bodmin Road it was all single track with passing loops, together with the necessity of reversals at Exeter, Wadebridge, Bodmin and Bodmin Road. Passengers being more mobile than parcels and freight, it was envisaged that most of the passenger trains would run as normally as possible between Penzance and Saltash, and between Plymouth North Road and Bristol or Paddington, but passengers would have to make their own way down to the Saltash ferry. On the St Budeaux (Devon) side a bus was to be provided - and a lorry for heavy luggage - to take them to North Road station. However, they would only connect there with the next departure and not with the one they had left at Saltash, as a separate train would leave North Road for Bristol or Paddington at its normal time.

Two passenger trains each day were to be diverted over the Southern Railway route - in the down direction the 10.30 am and 1.30 pm from Paddington, and up from Penzance the 9.30 am and 7.20 pm, each load to be a maximum of seven coaches. But the bulk of the traffic to be diverted over the North Cornwall line was goods, in trains not longer than 28 wagons plus two guard's vans, seven of which were scheduled each way each weekday, with up to 16 on Sundays.

Milk and clay trains were run only on Sundays, but the overnight Postal and Newspaper trains ran every day, together with parcels and perishable traffic - four up and three down.

The largest GWR engines allowed over this route would have been the 'Saint' Class 4-6-0s, but the bulk of the traffic would have been handled by 'Moguls' and either '45xx' or '51xx' 2-6-2Ts assisted by 'Bulldog' 4-4-0s. Banking and shunting engines were to be supplied at Boscarne Junction and Bodmin respectively, and all normal passenger services to Bodmin were to be replaced by buses for the duration of the emergency.

Happily, the foreseen emergency never materialised - but at least the GWR was ready.

13 January 1990

Goodrington Sands Halt

The 7.30 am Saturday express from Paddington to Kingswear is double-headed out of Goodrington Sands Halt by 4-6-0s Nos 4992 *Crosby Hall* and 1000 *County of Middlesex* on 9 July 1955. The latter still has its original design of double chimney, far more elegant than the new shorter double chimneys with which the whole class were modified during the next year or so.

When first seen at Hollacombe, at 2.30 pm that afternoon, only *County of Middlesex* was in charge of this 10-coach train, which was being held pending the clearance of a previous train from the down platform at Paignton station. On my arrival at Sands Road at 2.43 pm the offending stock was still in the down platform, with Paignton station pilot engine 2-6-2T No 5500 waiting for instructions where to go! Meanwhile, a furious argument ensued between the signalman in Paignton South box and the shunter as to what they should do with this empty stock.

The summer of 1955 was the last before additional carriage sidings were installed alongside Goodrington Sands Halt, and with the ever-increasing holiday traffic of the 1950s the staff were being put into an impossible position with increasing regularity on peak Saturdays.

However, on this particular day the situation resolved itself, as first 4-6-0 No 7027 *Thornbury Castle* came out of the yard and into the station with the 2.40 pm to Paddington, followed by 4-6-0 No 4958 *Priory Hall* on the 2.50 pm to Wolverhampton, and 4-6-0 No 6994 *Baggrave Hall* on the stock for the 3.05 pm to Wolverhampton.

With three roads in the yard now clear, No 5500 was able to proceed out of the station and over Sands Road crossing and into the yard, clearing the down line for the 7.30 am from Paddington, after holding it up for at least 20 minutes. Quite where 4-6-0 No 4992 *Crosby Hall* materialised from my note-book does not record, but that she was urgently needed at Kingswear there was no doubt, because she passed me on Goodrington bank at 3.11 pm, and returned from Kingswear - needless to say a little late - on the 3.20 pm from Kingswear to Cardiff, arriving back at Goodrington at 4.07 pm.

Goodrington Sands Halt originally opened in July 1928 when it was called Goodrington and had only one platform on the down side. It became Goodrington Sands in 1929, and in 1930 a second platform on the up side was added as part of a much larger scheme for the extension of the railway facilities at Paignton, which included the new Goods Depot in Dartmouth Road and the carriage sidings alongside. Although work was well advanced on further developments at the outbreak of war, particularly at Goodrington, nothing further was done until the winter of 1955-56, when the Tanners Lane level crossing became an overbridge, Goodrington Sands Halt booking office was opened on the bridge and the Happy Valley sidings were completed. The planned five-platform station at Paignton, which would have extended beneath an overbridge at Sands Road, would have solved many of the capacity problems encountered during the mid-1950s, but work on this had barely started in 1939, and was not to be resumed.

Goodrington Sands Halt was never closed as a British Rail station, but operation of it was transferred from British Rail to the preserved Dart Valley Railway at the end of 1972. Apart from the war years it has always been open only in the summer, although from 1951 to 1962 this extended from early May until late September. Goodrington Sands today is open from Easter to the end of October, when the trains run, manned by volunteer members of the Torbay & Dartmouth Railway Society.

20 January 1990

Wash-out!

In the autumn of 1960 week followed week with yet more rain, culminating in the disastrous flooding of the Exe and Culm valleys on 27 October that led to the substantial flood prevention works carried out through Exeter a few years later.

This picture was taken on the previous Saturday, 22 October 1960, from what was then the A38 Exeter Bypass at Countess Weir, and shows ex-GWR 'Castle' Class 4-6-0 No 4037 *The South Wales Borderers* storming along on the down Swansea to Penzance express with floodwater lapping the ballast on either side of the track. Clearly the Exe valley floodplain was already awash, and further rain could only mean disaster.

Earlier that month flooding had already caused problems at Plympton - a notorious spot in those days, where the railway tracks went underwater whenever there was heavy rainfall - and the Southern had had a bridge washed out near Crediton, because of which the through Brighton to Plymouth train was diverted via Newton Abbot on 8 October.

Ballast had been washed out on the Hemyock line, and also on the Southern's Torrington to Halwill Junction line near Petrockstow. The Seaton branch had also been closed for a day because of flooding and on 18 October, following more rain, there was a landslide on the Sidmouth branch.

Further heavy rain fell on Wednesday 26 October, causing immediate problems on the main line at Hele & Bradninch, while flooding also occurred on the Yeovil, Barnstaple and Minehead branches and in the Exe valley.

However, it was when this water reached the Exeter area on the Thursday that most damage was done. In those days the old Southern line from Crediton joined the Western main line at Cowley Bridge Junction on a low plate girder bridge over the river Exe. By midday the waters of the Exe were starting to back up behind the girders of this bridge, spilling out on to the Western main line and flowing down it under the road bridge and on towards Riverside yard.

The last up train to pass that day was the 'Torbay Express' behind 4-6-0 No 4098 *Kidwelly Castle*, while in the opposite direction the Southern's Plymouth to Brighton train behind 4-6-2 No 34011 *Tavistock* trod gingerly through the rising water, already well over rail level at 1.00 pm.

After that, with ballast likely to be washed out and odd timbers, barrels and fence-posts floating merrily down towards St David's station, the line was closed. By mid-afternoon, with St David's full of trains and the water level up to the coach axleboxes in the station, the principal Western trains were diverted over the Southern line - the up 'Cornish Riviera' left behind Southern 'Pacific' No 34024 *Tamar Valley*, travelling via Salisbury and Basingstoke. The down 'Torbay Express' came via Yeovil Pen Mill and Junction behind 4-6-0 No 4945 *Milligan Hall* and was eventually admitted to Exeter St David's station at 8.30 pm.

It was quite an exciting day - but one that the residents of the lower-lying parts of Exeter would doubtless rather forget.

10 February 1990

Index of locations